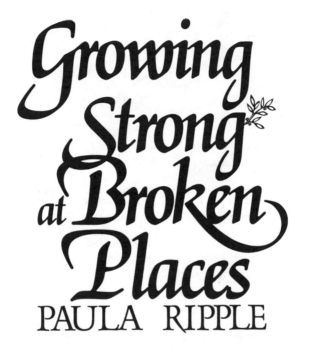

Growing Strong at Broken Places

PAULA RIPPLE

AVE MARIA PRESS   NOTRE DAME, INDIANA 46556

First printing, August, 1986
Second printing, March, 1987
40,000 copies in print

Acknowledgments

From COLLECTED POEMS, Harper and Row, Copyright © 1971, 1940, 1945, 1968 by Edna St. Vincent Millay and Norma Millay Ellis.

Excerpts from "The Cocktail Party," "East Coker," and "Burnt Norton," from T. S. ELIOT: THE COMPLETE POEMS AND PLAYS, 1909-1950; Harcourt, Brace & World. Copyright © 1971, Esme Valerie Eliot.

Excerpts from THE NEW JERUSALEM BIBLE, copyright © 1985 by Darton, Longman and Todd, Ltd., and Doubleday & Company, Inc. Reprinted by permission of the publisher.

Author's Note
All quotations from scripture and other literary sources appear exactly according to the copyright versions. I was not free to change these, but made an effort to use inclusive language wherever else possible, However, I chose not to use he/she and other devices to avoid sexist language, finding that they break the flow of both the writing and the reading.

International Standard Book Number: 0-87793-340-5
0-87793-341-3 (pbk.)
Library of Congress Catalog Card Number: 86-71124
Cover and Text Design: Katherine A. Robinson
Printed and bound in the United States of America.

For Don,
my best friend and faithful companion,
who shares
the pain and the joy
of discovering
the moving still point of life.

Acknowledgments

Many people have had a part in the writing and publication of this book. To them I offer my gratitude. Special thanks to the following:

— Sister Patricia Alden, F.S.P.A., for her steady love and ongoing support.

— Sister Carola Unser, F.S.P.A., for reading the first drafts of several chapters and for offering both practical suggestions and affirming words.

— Scott, who never failed to ask how the book was coming and then reassured me with his smiles.

— Chris, whose presence made the difficult task of writing a much less lonely one.

— Jack Finnegan, a faithful friend, who has taught me the meaning of perseverance in suffering.

— Father Thomas Gedeon and Father Robert Pelton, for their strong personal and professional support.

— Other friends whose tested love of many years has been both challenging and unconditional.

— The Franciscan Sisters of Perpetual Adoration who have shared the journey through suffering to renewed life.

If I had to choose
between
pain and no feeling,
I would choose pain.

William Faulkner

Contents

Introduction

. . . It takes
So many thousand years to wake,
But will you wake for pity's sake . . .
Wake up, will you?
                    A Sleep of Prisoners, Christopher Fry

The history of the human family reveals the truth that pain is a part of every human life. Neither power nor wealth, neither education nor ability, neither gifts of creativity nor stores of human energy can insure against the reality that suffering will be our companion at some time during our journey. It is a presence as inseparable from the human condition as food and oxygen are from human life. It is part of our legacy. Suffering is as unique as the genetic makeup of each person and as universal as our basic physical features.

We can perceive suffering as an intolerable companion or look at it as a guide leading us far beyond ourselves as it invites us to become more familiar with what is deep inside ourselves. Part of the mystery of suffering is that it lacks its fullest meaning until we have taken time to reflect on, and somehow bring together, both that outer and inner experience.

You might question the wisdom of choosing pain, suffering or adversity as the subject of a book. Who wants to take time to dwell on a topic about which we may already have too much information that is not helpful, that offers no possibility of removing it permanently from life?

If I understood and could explain better the suffering that has been a part of my own life, perhaps I would not be drawn to the difficult task of articulating the various aspects of suffering that are a part of the lives of most of the friends I have known well.

In a recent, painful encounter with a friend who called to my attention that he did not believe I was living all that I had written about in my book on friendship, a somewhat obvious insight came to mind. I realized that my effort to reflect some of the major themes about relationships that seemed important to me was also an effort to clarify those ideas for myself. The willingness to share those ideas with others, linked with the awareness of my responsibility to be clear and faithful to what I believed, created the tension out of which arose the energy essential to sustain the process. Authors often select those very topics with which they are still wrestling as the subject matter of their reflections.

I found this thought reinforced by G.K. Chesterton writing in *Orthodoxy*:

> . . . It is very hard for a man to defend anything of which he is entirely convinced. It is comparatively easy when he is only partially convinced. He is partially convinced because he has found this or that proof of the thing, and he can expound it. But a man is not really convinced of a philosophic theory when he finds that something proves it . . .
>
> . . . There is, therefore, about all complete conviction a kind of huge helplessness. The belief is so big that it takes a long time to get it into action. And this hesitation chiefly arises, oddly enough, from an indifference about where one should begin. All roads lead to Rome; which is one reason why many people never get there.

Partly because of the ambiguity expressed by Chesterton, and partly out of experiences that have been undeniably clear to me, I approach the subject of suffering.

I remember as a child asking my mother why Jesus had to be treated so badly by people to whom he had offered only love and healing. As a teenager I wondered why life was not more fair, why effort was not necessarily rewarded. I continue to recognize that the creator who loves us made many promises which have been faithfully kept, but there was no promise that life would be "fair."

I was fortunate to have learned long ago that God does not punish us with the various forms of suffering that are a part of life. But, I have no way of resolving the question, "Is suffering necessary to greater life, or is its presence a goad that might be replaced with a more amiable stimulant?" As a Christian, I am well aware of the clear statements of Jesus. As an idealist, I continue to speculate on the possible impact on human life and growth in a lifelong environment of unconditional acceptance. We have such love from God, but what would life be like for us if we could offer it to one another?

Asking the questions about what a pain-free life would be like does not remove from me the conviction that our national pursuit of a pain-free way is close to the sources of our destruction. I wonder about the implications of John Steinbeck's statement that "no culture has ever been comfortable, wealthy and powerful and survived." Jacob Needleman voiced this same opinion in another way when he wrote in *The Way of the Physician*, "It is not possible for man to become both comfortable and conscious at the same time."

If we are preoccupied with running from pain, we are not likely to discover the meaning that might be found in running with our pain, in staying with it and entering into it. Let me be clear about the fact that we are called neither to seek it out nor to revel in it. But, when pain is present there is also some call to discover some new facet of life.

When overprotective parents seek to provide an environment that is free from hardship, they deprive their children of life experiences without which they will not grow. When people in counseling and other healing professions cannot tolerate the presence of pain in the life of a client, they become agents of destruction rather than of growth. The promise of instant pain removal is not therapeutic in the long-distance run toward a more complete life.

None of us is totally and consistently present to our own life. Each of us is, at some time, a sleepwalker, lacking full awareness of the life possibilities that might be discovered. Suffering is one of the ways through which we are awakened. It is like the persistent caller at the door, sometimes in the day and sometimes in the dark of night.

Paul's words, "Wake up, sleeper, rise from the dead" (Eph 5:14), are a reminder that the sleepwalkers among us will never experience the fullness of life's potential.

Defining the Terms

Having had to plunge in somewhere to begin these reflections on the place of and the meaning to be found in human pain, I want to set the context for the chapters that follow.

This book will deal with physical pain in only one chapter because I cannot write about it from my own experience and because I believe that physical pain can have meaning only if it is set in the context of a wider consideration of the meaning of human suffering.

A distinction is sometimes made between physical and moral suffering. I have chosen not to follow that distinction because of what I believe to be the connotations on the word "moral" among us. To link sin and judgment to all suffering is to reinforce an ancient question that Jesus sought to put to rest when he was asked about the man born blind, "Who has sinned, this man or his parents, for him to have been born blind?" His answer does not deny the fact that men and women do sin and that suffering comes into the world as a result of sinful lives. Jesus makes a powerful case that the association of sin with suffering ought not be automatically made when he responds with, "Neither he nor his parents sinned, he was born blind so that the works of God might be revealed in him" (Jn 9:3).

I prefer to define physical suffering as the suffering of the body, the hurts of the flesh, and to distinguish that from all of the other forms of human suffering — the suffering of the spirit, the hurts of the heart, the afflictions of the human psyche in its quest for a more meaningful and more deeply rooted life.

With great respect for those who know the experience of physical suffering in ways not yet known to me, I believe that all suffering is somehow related and that no form is totally isolated from others. Found in all suffering is a call to discover both the life that is yet hidden in us and to seek the life that is outside waiting to be experienced. We suffer as wayfarers on the human journey because there is evil in the world around us. We suffer from our own sinfulness and that of others. We suffer from the evil that exists in governments and in other institutions.

As individuals who sometimes sleepwalk through portions of the journey that is ours, we will experience the pain of seeking

—to grow up, to somehow make it through our adolescence, at whatever age this occurs

—to know and cherish ourselves more completely

—to accept the human condition as the gift of the creator and embrace it as Jesus did

—to be capable of friendship and to seek to remove the obstacles to loving others well

—to have the courage to stand alone when our convictions necessitate it

—to accept change as a basis for all life, personal and institutional

—to be open to the risk involved in making life decisions

— to deal with differences, however personally threatening they may be

— to search for our way in new and yet undiscovered territory, whether inside or outside of us

— to value self-reflection and prayer for the costly and rewarding process that it is

— to seek forgiveness for ourselves and to offer it to others

— to share our suffering and recognize it as a common denominator between ourselves and others.

In these and countless other ways, we recognize the pain that is involved in becoming more responsive and present to our own lives. We are at once surprised and distressed by the persistent presence of a companion that we will come to know and from whom we cannot escape. We must eventually replace Job's question, "Why do good men and women suffer?" with the question, "How do I enter into my suffering?"

In the coming chapters we will reflect on suffering's countless and unpredicted sources. With its many forms and faces, it intrudes into the ordinary, as well as the extraordinary, events of life. It rises out of the obvious as well as the imperceptible changes we face. It is as present in our desire for sure answers as it is in our search for life-giving questions. It haunts us in our efforts to struggle with forgiving and being forgiven. It challenges us in our mysterious journey to self-discovery and shared intimacy.

Its sources surprise us with their persistent intensity. The process of awakening to life is never separate from some experience of pain.

When we are fully awake and open to our lives, we will not experience less pain, but we will gradually cherish ourselves enough to want the deepest experiences of life that we can have. In retrospect we will know and believe that every step of the way has a role to play in fashioning who we are and who we can become. The price of this knowing is high.

> The hallowing of Pain
> Like the hallowing of Heaven,
> Obtains as a corporeal cost—
> The Summit is not given
>
> To Him who strives severe—
> At middle of the Hill—
> But He who has achieved the Top—
> All—is the price of All—
>
> *The Hallowing of Pain,* Emily Dickinson

1 Awakening to Life: A Costly Venture

One learns of the pain of others by suffering one's own
pain, by turning inside oneself, by finding one's own
soul. It is important to know of pain. It destroys
our self-pride, our arrogance, our indifference toward others.
The Chosen, Chaim Potok

Discovering the meaning of suffering is similar to understanding other human experiences. No matter how perceptive we may be, we know that the greater the distance between ourselves and that which we seek to understand, the less likely we will be to grasp all its implications.

We gain some understanding of an event or of some aspect of life through reading about it. We may come closer through speaking to someone who was a witness. But there is no substitute for experiencing the event firsthand.

We cannot experience another's suffering as that person does. But there are universal truths that make it possible for us to identify with the sufferings of others if we have suffered ourselves and reflected on its meaning. Edna St. Vincent Millay writes, "Count them unclean, these tears that turn no mill." Tears that "turn no mill" give witness to the tragedy of pain that has lost one of its redeeming features; pain cannot really be shared unless it has been reflected upon and some of its meaning revealed to the one who has suffered. Discovering and sharing the common denominators of pain is the basis for self-help groups as Alcoholics Anonymous, support groups for the separated and divorced, and the bonds that form between families who have lost a young child to the ravages of cancer.

We speak of thresholds of pain, the ability to tolerate pain. We observe that because life is not fair, people do not suffer in the same way — either in quantity or intensity. We are led to ask questions about the breaking points, about the places of desolation and despair in which we find ourselves.

I have often asked, "Why does the same form of suffering lead some to self-destruction and others to renewed life?" It is true that we can never see the insides of another's life as that person does. It is clear that no two people, even in the same family, have the same human history. Yet we wonder about the different responses to situations that bear a significant number of common denominators.

In his poem "Easter," Yeats first says, "He, too, has been changed in turn,/Transformed utterly: A terrible beauty is born." He offers these words as description of the change in a man he had earlier called "a drunken, vainglorious lout." This is poetic testimony to the redemptive, life-giving power of adversity.

But later in that same poem, the plaguing question we have posed is framed in these words, "Too long a sacrifice/Can make of the heart a stone."

We cannot directly prepare ourselves for tragedy and suffering. By its very nature, it is unpredictable and finds us scurrying to find the inner resources out of which to respond. It challenges our faith in God's ever present love for us and often forces us to reach out to others for a steadying hand. We are awakened to life in unexpected ways.

As we walk in experiences foreign to us, we have the possibility of discovering gifts and goodness, strengths and courage that had never been tested. We may recognize, eventually with a sense of gratitude, that necessity has pushed us where virtue never led us.

Unforeseen and seemingly life-shattering experiences — such as the death of a loved one, the loss of a marriage through separation and divorce, the discovery of a hidden and far-advanced cancer, the loss of position and economic security, the running away from home of a teenage son or daughter — in some unique way push us relentlessly to rely on resources yet hidden even from us. We are all much stronger than we know; we are all capable of more courageous decisions than any we have yet made. Looking back over their shoulder at some experience of intense adversity, we hear people say, "I never would have believed that I could have made it."

Many lives give witness to the profound Christian belief that life follows death, but who of us has not met someone for whom this is not true. The same suffering which eventually deepens and beautifies one life may leave another in bitterness and self-isolation. Are there some keys to the life after death of which we speak? Are there some ways of insuring our own responses when pain seeks us out?

Recognizing the Roots of Suffering

One of the greatest places of revelation of the various forms and faces of human suffering for me has been in directing retreats. I discovered that regardless of the theme selected and the scriptural base of the reflections, the questions that became central were most often related to the areas where people were experiencing pain in some form or another. Out of their discomfort, sometimes out of their fear and insecurity, people's concerns, doubts and dreams were enfleshed in words, most often in questions. And these questions were most often related to the inner movements of their lives. In all the retreats I have directed, whether for married couples, young people not married, religious, widows and widowers, or divorcing people, we always got back to what I have come to think of as some basic roadblocks to life where varying amounts of pain arise.

The questions have no priority. They just arise when people come together to share their journeys and to reach beyond themselves for new and renewed life. These are questions that are asked out of varied personal histories and differing types of education. The questions are almost always the subject of concern and the source of pain.

What is religion?

Who is God?

What does it mean to be created human?

What is sin?

What is prayer?

How do we deal with the threefold nature of relationships? My relationship with myself? With others? With God?

Why do human beings suffer? Why some more than others?

Where/What are heaven and hell?

Where does evil come from?

My 13 years' experience working with the separated and divorced taught me that what really needed to be dealt with was more than that experience. Divorce was the vehicle that made people, perhaps for the first time, deal with lifelong unresolved questions about their faith, their misshapen images of God, their undue fears of punishment and their underdeveloped sense of personal responsibility for making decisions that can lead to the full life to which God's love calls us.

We discover that often people cannot even shape the life-giving questions because they are looking for answers. Sometimes they are not ready to ask and respond to the questions that will lead to life. What is revealed is the inner suffering that results from falsely formed insights into these key questions which, in turn, makes it either more difficult or nearly impossible for good people to deal with the outsides of their lives.

For example, it is nearly impossible to facilitate life for any person who believes that every form of adversity is some response of a God lying in wait to punish. People may be broken by failure when they refuse to come to terms with the fact that to be human is to sometimes fail and that no form of failure is an end unless we choose to believe that it is. For those who have come to terms with the realities of being human, failure can be a place of beginning again and in more meaningful ways.

My experience leads me to the conviction that natural disasters such as destructive earthquakes and hurricanes, disease and death are not as potentially destructive of the human person as the set of questions that we have been discussing. We will deal with these outer forces, however profound their impact, if we come to terms with the questions that are at the core of our existence. It is at the central place of life that decisions are born which determine the kind of persons we shall be.

The Message in the Lives of Others

It is not enough for us to recognize that we share a common brokenness as sharers of the human journey. Giving personal testimonial to our own wounds is not enough, for lives simply broken do not necessarily enrich the lives of others and may not lead to richer and renewed life for the person in pain. Only when our pain is somehow internalized in a meaningful way does it have the possibility of bringing us to some new place of life and then allowing us to offer that new life to others. Suffering may seem to break us, but unless our lives are not only broken but broken into, we shed "tears that turn no mill," we endure pain that is not redemptive for ourselves and others. We need the message of the lives of others who have gone before or who walk with us now. We need the assurance of those whose lives have been broken into that suffering is a companion that we first fear, then come to understand, and much later, cherish and embrace. We rejoice in our greater awareness of the meaning of life and would not wish to return to the world of the sleepwalkers.

We wish to grow beyond the childhood of unbroken dreams, beyond the restlessness of adolescence, to a place of inner integrity and openness to the never-ending change that is a rich and beautiful (albeit costly) dimension of full human life.

I have never been able to identify with Paul's invitation in Colossians 1:24 to be "happy to be suffering" while I was struggling through it. At times of intense pain the primary call we seem to hear and to which we respond is to survive, to make it through. As a friend has often said to me, "Just keep on keeping on."

Reading about the lives of those who have suffered is one way of walking through suffering that has not yet come to us. Talking to someone who has suffered well can be a profound and life-giving invitation to learn about this companion whose face seems harsh and unattractive. But, the meaning of suffering is in the suffering. There are some things we cannot internalize through the experiences of others. All of the study of sociological systems, the conversations about breakdown necessarily preceding breakthrough, seem to lose their logic when it is our job that is on the line, when it is our profession that is undergoing profound changes over which we have no control. At some point in our lives, we discover that the next step flows from the preceding one and we are not comfortable with being out of control, powerless to resist the current carrying us to some new place of life.

The experience of powerlessness is another facet of suffering. For people who have lived well-ordered lives and for whom every well-thought-through decision carried with it the expectation of predictable advancement and success, powerlessness is not a welcome teacher.

I remember vividly the warnings I listened to as I drove

along Highway 36 between Minneapolis and St. Paul. The radio announcer was reminding us that there were severe thunderstorms predicted. As the rain began, gently at first, I was secure in that I did not have far to go and that I had driven through thunderstorms before. I arrived home as the heaviest rain began to fall and was happy to be secure and dry inside my apartment. When I turned on the television to watch the late evening news, the warnings about thunderstorms in the area were repeated. Then, the light began to flicker so I lit a candle and unplugged the TV. Before I could close the patio drapes, the wind became so intense that it seemed to rock the whole building.

As I hurried to close the drapes, there was what seemed to be a final and most powerful wind, then a loud crack. The next thing I remember was someone knocking on my door asking, "Are you all right?" I did not know that a tornado had made its way directly through and had totally destroyed a shopping mall, an apartment complex of several buildings next door, and had ripped the roof off most of our building.

It was only the next day when the police, who were guarding against looting in the area, allowed me to walk beyond our complex that I realized more of what had happened. When I looked at the twisted frames of large brick structures, I wondered how anyone had gotten out of those buildings alive. When I was told that the wind had picked up a car and dropped it several blocks away, I remembered how close I had been to my glass doors just seconds before the tornado took our roof.

I remember walking back to my apartment, the only one in my building which had been protected from the torrential rains that followed the twister, feeling as though my legs could not support me. I was panicky at my own stupidity in having stood, immobile, right in the place the shattered glass patio doors could have landed (as they had done in the apartment across the hall.)

That night I read the newspaper account of the storm, looked at the pictures and read the statistics. My first thought was to wonder why the reporters had not done a better job of portraying the actual events and the magnitude of the impact for those of us who lived there.

Later a friend called and I felt frustrated and somewhat hurt at the seeming lack of concern for what I had been through. I felt as helpless to describe how I still felt inside as I was to give him an adequate picture of how different my neighborhood would be on his next visit.

The media could describe the physical damage, but it could not get inside the feelings of people who had to leave their homes and all of their possessions to seek shelter.

I could tell my friend how I had felt, but he could not share in what that experience had meant to me. Even a week later, when we walked through the ruins of the buildings next door, I could not communicate to him and he could not understand what that night had been like for those of us who lived there.

And so it is with the various forms of suffering that are a part of life, reading about them, hearing about and surviving them are vastly different experiences.

So our search for role models, reading about the lives of others, hearing from them their accounts of unique forms of suffering bravely borne, is not enough, but it is helpful.

Common Misconceptions About Pain

Until we come to terms with the widespread belief that every form of suffering is always destructive and must be removed as quickly as possible, we will continue to expend large amounts of money and even greater amounts of human effort to avoid or run away from it. Investing our energy in learning how to deal with it — how to respond to the hidden call to new life inside the experiences of pain — will better serve us.

Those who claim to be able to remove pain quickly rob us of the lessons to be learned from our own pain so that we might allow it to get inside ourselves, there to create the tension out of which a more awakened life might arise.

There are those who would tell us that pain is always and only an inconvenience for life, one with which we ought never have to deal. They claim that suffering is a chronic distress without redeeming features. They mislead us into believing that we can manipulate God. They also forget the very important fact that God loves us too much and respects human freedom too much to free us, magically, from the pain that is involved in growing as we make the journey of life.

Those who claim power as their god live out of the belief that, if you know the right people and have the proper position, you can avoid the suffering that is the lot of ordinary human beings. They refuse to accept the fact that there are some things that cannot be bought and sold just as there are some life realities that no one can hire removed.

Jesus made it abundantly clear that mustard seeds had to go deep into the ground to discover life, that the grain of wheat had to die, and that men and women had burdens to carry in exchange for the promises of life to the full.

Out of the wisdom of the eastern religious traditions comes the adage that, "When the pupil is ready, the teacher will come." There is no better preparation for the advent of life's best teachers than the tempering of our lives through suffering which prepares us to hear for the first time messages that may have been around us before.

The Rewards of Suffering Well

In order to respond to the call to love God and our neighbor as ourselves, there are obstacles to be removed, gifts to be discovered, limitations to be dealt with. We search for both our inner depths and our outermost margins. Love warms and nurtures this process, but, I believe that it is suffering that sets the process in motion. Dreams are born in discontent. Coming to believe this with my head is one step, but embracing suffering for its life-giving possibilities means that my head and my heart are joined. With head and heart joined, we might share Rainer Maria Rilke's sentiments:

> I love the dark hours of my being
> in which the senses drop into the deep.
> I have found in them, as in old letters,
> my private life. . . .

When we have gained new insights into ourselves, insights which, when shared, widen our understanding of all of life, we have reaped a rich reward for our tears.

When we share our suffering, we are bonded in unique ways to others who have suffered. We speak a common language, a language foreign to those for whom the escape from pain is a major life project.

Well-borne suffering tempers the human spirit, gentles us in our approach and response to others. It makes of us able emissaries of the sometimes subtle and mysterious messages of life. Because suffering is itself a mystery, reflecting on its meaning helps us unlock the key to other mysteries we encounter in the process of learning to live, and helps us be more willing to take the risks involved in sharing the life we have discovered.

Something about suffering expands the margins of our world and helps us reach into the worlds of others far from our own. Paul describes the process of coming to new life as one of groaning and stretching. We are called to stretch to find the strength we need to bear the sufferings that are ours. Having found that we can reach farther than we knew, we are called to repeat that process with different people and in differing situations.

We have spoken of suffering as a process that can make us more sensitive and responsive to others, but it can increase our ability to love even as we may become more lovable. Recognizing (with Dostoevsky) that "love in dreams is easy but

real love is a harsh and dreadful reality," we know that suffering well is one of the keys to loving relationships.

When suffering prods us to let go of some of the obstacles to life that have been a part of our lives for a long time,
there is more space in us for life itself. In the suffering of powerlessness and helplessness, we reach to God who is our primary source of strength, and we reach to one another. We also
discover that, even in our moments of powerlessness, we can
yet be present for someone who reaches to us.

Even the history of the gods and goddesses of ancient
times reveals the presence of suffering that at once threatened
to destroy and to reveal new life.

One of my favorite myths is the story of Ariadne. Her
response to her pain can serve as a message of life for us.

When Theseus returns from Athens to Crete, he is given
the message that he must pass through the labyrinth of the
underworld to slay the minotaur. Frightened at the prospect of
this fearsome journey, he enlists the support of Ariadne who
agrees to hold a thread so that Theseus can both enter the
complicated and threatening labyrinth and then find his way
out. In return for this favor, Theseus promises his friend,
Ariadne, that he will take her with him from Crete.

Theseus is successful in his ventures into the labyrinth
and so he and his friend Ariadne sail from Crete. On the first
night of their journey, they stop on the island of Naxos. The
next morning, Theseus slips quietly away without Ariadne.

When Ariadne awakens and discovers that she has been
abandoned by him whose future she helped make secure, she
feels abandoned and betrayed. In her desperation she says, "I
will never love again; I will never live again."

Forced by a situation that she cannot change, Ariadne
somehow discovers that her relationship with Theseus was that
of a protector, not that of a friend, companion and lover. In
the face of the loss of Theseus, and with the agony of rejection
and loss heavy upon her, she discovers more about herself,
more about her way of being friend to Theseus, and she is
forced to confront her ways of caring.

Theseus must abandon Ariadne to discover more about himself, to learn more about faithfulness to life and to relationship.

In letting go of the thread that has protected Theseus, Ariadne is invited to let go of the bonds that were more like those of mother and son than of friends and lovers, bonds that would have allowed her to remain less aware, less awake to the life that was possible both for her and for Theseus.

The thread to which Ariadne must cling and be faithful is that which will lead her into her own center, will lead her to the possibility of loving and being loved.

Her proclamation, "I will never love again; I will never live again" is not an end but a beginning for her. It prepares her to accept the love of Dionysos, the only god who does not exploit females, the only god who is faithful as a husband.

This simple and profound story summarizes both the intensity of pain that can be experienced and the rich life that can flow from pain reflected upon.

If the task of growing through suffering is sometimes the simple act of holding on and making it to some new possible place of life, then the reward is the greater awareness of what life can mean.

Jesus had no window into the peace and joy of Easter as he wrestled with the agony of his Good Friday.

The only insurance that we can be like Jesus (or like Ariadne) is that we enter into our suffering as we strive to enter into life each day, to accept what we cannot control or decide, and then to grow to some new place of life.

Time does go on —
I tell it gay to those who suffer now —
They shall survive —
There is a sun —
They don't believe it now —
                    Time Does Go On, Emily Dickinson

2 Nourished by Our Daily Bread

Yes! to this thought I hold with firm persistence
The last result of wisdom stamps it true;
He only earns his freedom and existence
Who daily conquers them anew.

Faust, Goethe

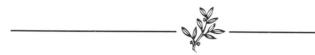

A few years ago pictures of such famous presidents as Lincoln, Theodore Roosevelt, Kennedy and Johnson were shown on television, contrasting each man before and after his presidency. The commentary spoke of the ways in which their years in the White House had profoundly changed the facial appearance of each man.

As the significant events of their terms of office were recounted, the point was made that probably neither the man nor his family nor his closest associates were aware of the changes as they were occurring.

Certainly the day-to-day changes in each of our lives are much the same. A person living with a young child will not notice the differences apparent to someone who goes a few weeks without seeing that same child. As we grow older, noticeable changes take much longer, but the effect is there. Small changes that are neither perceptible nor measurable take place.

What is true of individuals is also true of institutions, nations and cultures. Herbert Hendin, in his book *The Age of Sensation,* presents us with this same reality when he says that changes in cultures and governments cause personal changes we may be unaware of until something outside ourselves focuses our attention on what is going on inside of us.

Sometimes a single fact or statistic can call our attention to changes that have been going on for a long time and to a degree we have not yet considered. Such a statistic for me was a statement in a professional journal that only 7 percent of today's American families fit the traditional model so familiar a decade or two ago—that is, a mother whose primary responsibility is the home and family and who has no outside job, and a father who provides for the family's economic well-being. When we reflect on such a change in a societal unit, or other changes such as the impact of increased mobility, a longer life span, or new roles for women, we realize they all have an impact on each one of us and our way of life.

To use a different image, the changes that enliven or destroy a relationship often occur imperceptibly. Small responses to the demands of intimacy between two people or corresponding failure to respond will eventually result in either bridges or walls set in nearly unnoticed ways. And walls between two people are like the stone walls of the New England countryside — they are set stone by stone, step by step, and can be removed only in the same way.

Cardinal John Newman once said that to live is to change, and to grow is to have changed many times. We come to understand that life often seeks to enter into us without our notice and that we are not able to measure the growth that may be taking place. We can set time-lapse cameras to clock the short-term changes in plants; we can measure our own growth in height and weight over a period of time, but we have no such means of revealing the inner life that is at the heart of determining who we are and who we are becoming.

Christians speak of the process of conversion. The word of God and the life of Jesus are ongoing invitations to grow toward the fullness of life offered by a loving creator. But, like the weathering of rocks or leaves turning toward the sunlight, the process of conversion is gradual and never finished. What seems a sudden change to others is perceived more gradually in the day-to-day changes of the individual.

Too Familiar to Be Important

It is important for us to give serious thought to the importance of the nearly unnoticed change that results from decisions so familiar as to be made almost automatically. We may come to respond out of habit rather than conviction or commitment. We may even be aware of what we are doing but decide that it is too small to be consequential.

A single word, while it may evoke poetic images, is not yet a poem. The precise choice of words set carefully in relationship to one another makes a poem.

A single stroke of an artist's brush does not make a work of art. Adding stroke to stroke eventually results in the emergence of a figure on the canvas. Someone has described the process of human life as the continual selection of appropriate colors and brushes that results in the creation of a human personality. When the work is completed, the individual choices may not be either remembered or discernible but we know that the choices were many.

In our age of hype and heightened expectations of bigger and better productions in all areas of life, it is not surprising that we risk losing a sense of the value of the small and the nearly unnoticed channels through which life also comes to us.

It is the nature of human life that we do not usually progress by yards and miles, we do not run with lightning speed toward the new and undiscovered possibilities. Most of the time we inch our way toward life, gaining insights slowly and opening ourselves cautiously to yet unsampled challenges.

Just as we may feel more sure of our ability to respond to a major crisis than to deal with life's daily monotonies, so we may forget the importance of valuing the choices we make many times each day. In his *Courage to Create*, Rollo May says:

But a man or woman becomes fully human only by his choices and his commitment to them. People attain worth and dignity by the multitude of decisions they make from day to day.

The gospel reminds us that Jesus consistently drew his most powerful images of the meaning of life from the familiar things and events that surrounded and were a part of his human journey. His parables are uncomplicated descriptions of familiar circumstances and experiences in the lives of those who shared his journey. He used the mustard seed and the precious pearl, the man born blind and the powerful tax collector to tell us of the life that is and the life that can come to be.

Discovering the New in the Familiar

If we hope to continue to value those things that are a part of our daily lives, it is important for us to search for new meaning in the familiar. The effort required is well rewarded when we catch new glimpses of meaning in what we risk losing due to overfamiliarity, or when we realize that because we have changed, we are able to see that which was once unnoticed.

Some examples of this experience are as follows:

1. We read a book or poem that we have read before or see a movie we have seen before and we discover that it has an entirely new meaning for us—almost as though we had not read or seen it before.

2. We meet an old friend and have a different experience from any other meeting—we notice things about the friend and about our responses that we had not noticed or felt before.

3. We examine and reflect on our values and discover we

are not in the same place we once were. Our values may have changed or our priority with regard to those values may have shifted.

4. We realize that many things which were once painful or a source of feeling response now no longer are.

5. We visit a city and we are attracted by a whole different set of places and experiences there.

6. We remember things that were once very important and we realize that they no longer are.

7. We meet people we once had very little in common with and suddenly experience the possibility of important bonds.

8. Family or friends tell us stories about how we once were and we realize that what they are telling us is true but that we are different now.

9. We read something we have written and we feel inside as though we are reading someone else's words.

10. What we once worked very hard for is no longer important and we now invest our energies somewhere else for different reasons.

11. We look at pictures of ourselves and can hardly identify with the person we see.

Finding new meaning is like discovering the hidden shapes of animal and human profiles in the ever-changing clouds. Just as cloud-watching requires concentration and imagination, so avoiding the boredom of rapidly passing and similar days requires attentiveness to our lives and nourishment of our creative powers.

No detail of life is insignificant, no decision too unimportant to have far-reaching implications. At the heart of the inner attitudes out of which we make choices rests the stance that we ultimately take toward life. Out of the fabric woven by the threads of each day is created the tapestry of our life. Subtle hues may be those that give depth and beauty to the images revealed as the picture grows more complete.

Words of Those Open to Change

The words of people who recognized the changes in their own lives remind us not only of the changes themselves but of the price we pay. To take responsibility for one's life in such a way as to be aware of change and its implications; to be conscious of the cumulative effect of daily decisions is to feel the cost of life.

Lewis Carroll speaks of the kind of change we are considering and of its association with our journey in self-discovery.

"Who are you?" asked the caterpillar. "I hardly know, sir, just at the present," replied Alice shyly, "at least I know who I was when I got up this morning, but I think I must have changed several times since then."

Charles Darwin, throughout his writings, stated that he had consistently made an effort to keep his mind so free that he would be ready to abandon any hypothesis, however important it had been to him, as soon as he found facts that could be shown to oppose it. He claimed that he could not remember any first-formed hypothesis which, after a time, had not been modified or given up.

And so it is with us in our effort to gain insights and to continue to refine our values as we give direction to our lives and internalize those values by which we will choose to live.

Gandhi said that before he spoke or wrote he tried not to think of what he might have said before. His goal was not to be consistent with any of his previous statements on a certain topic, but to live with such integrity that what he said was consistent with the truth as it continually presented itself to topic, but to live with such integrity that what he said was consistent with the truth as it continually presented itself to him.

Tolstoy believed that human life gradually destroys itself unless it is nourished with new experiences and fresh insights. He saw the destructiveness of isolation and the need for the pain that is involved in facing new challenges and responding with courage. He speaks of the "enemy" of complacence when he says, "All of you undisturbed cities, haven't you ever longed for the Enemy?"

The expansion of personal worlds often happens when something comes into our lives that stretches us beyond where we now are, something that causes some discomfort. The expansion happens when we care enough to see if we can discover where those feelings are coming from and what they are related to.

Accepting and even coming to cherish these disturbances as well as seeking to make friends with the "enemy" that intrudes are important ways of providing possible growth. They help prevent our world from becoming smaller than it is.

Lao-tse says that it is a wise man who looks into space and does not consider that which is small as being too little, nor that which is great as too big, for he believes that the dimensions of life are limitless.

Symbols That Speak to Us of Change

Searching for the symbolic meaning hidden in those things that surround us can help us become more aware of ever-present and inevitable change. These symbols grow more sacred and reveal more meaning as we make an effort to put words around them.

In recent years I realized I have lived much of my life in cities that were built around large rivers — Spokane, La Crosse, Wisconsin, Minneapolis and Boston. Most of those years were spent in a Mississippi River valley nestled between two ridges of bluffs.

Walking alongside a rapidly moving river, I have often been reminded of the many ways in which the current and the movement of the water are a powerful symbol of change. When I walk beside the river in a place where I can see both of the ridges of bluffs, I am struck by the contrast between the moving river and the unmoving bluffs. One a symbol of the changing and the other of the changeless, I think.

But, as I continue to contrast the river and the bluffs, I am gradually more aware of the seasonal changes in the foliage that covers the bluffs. When I drive or walk near them, I see large rocks that have fallen and small pieces that have broken off. The water trickles into crevices, freezes and serves as an effective agent in the weathering process that forms new soil. I come to realize that the bluffs are changing, too, but their change is less perceptible than the constant movement of the river they cast shadows on.

The evidence of the changeless is much more difficult to discover, the symbols of the unchanging much fewer in number. In retrospect I have often realized that changelessness may be falsely associated with change that may be so gradual as to be imperceptible at any given moment. Perhaps the river, because of its continual movement, is unchanging in its ever-changing nature, not unlike the life journey of every human person. How much of life is lost to us because we watch and wait for miracles while we fail to acknowledge the life that comes to us through the ebb and flow of ordinary days. We even allow life to pass us by while we wait for the future life we long for and dream of.

The Challenges of the Daily

St. John, speaking of the Eucharist, tells us that "Anyone who eats this bread will live forever" (Jn 6:58). The events and gifts that are a part of each day's life are our daily bread to the extent that we allow ourselves to be enriched and nourished by them.

This daily bread has the potential to nourish us if we are

committed to noticing the courage involved in making daily decisions well rather than in expecting to witness miracles.

But it takes effort to become open to life. Risks are involved in sampling this bread of daily existence. Obstacles to receiving the nourishment may be hidden in this daily bread.

On any given day we might be confronted with any one or more of the following possibilities:

Boredom. Because days may pass in rapid succession and because we may be less than alert to the richness of what is present even in the most ordinary, we lack excitement for what we look on as the monotonous repetition of tasks and events. We may decide that it takes too much effort to look for the possibilities that could be there.

Weariness. We human beings do get tired. We may give less and less of ourselves to each day. Gradually, we miss more of the life that can be ours because we see it as a spectator sport where we are entertained by the investment and involvement of others.

Drowsiness. Sometimes we are not only inattentive and uninvolved, but we are sleepwalkers. If we notice anything at all, it is either by accident or by some misfortune. We are sometimes not easily awakened; it may take some tragedy to finally catch our attention. Then, tragedy may push us where virtue never led us.

Survival. If the goal for our life is simply "making it through," we will miss much of the richness and goodness that can only be found in savoring the journey. Woody Allen is quoted as saying that "half of life is just making it through to Friday." Even if this is true, we still have to ask, "But what about the other half?"

It is important for us to have good survival skills in approaching the pitfalls and perils of life, but we are not called simply to survival. God's loving wish for us as Jesus says, is "Life to the full."

Insensitivity. Being tempered by life is very different from being traumatized or paralyzed by it. The very nature of repetition and familiarity with people and events carries with it the danger of becoming less and less sensitive, less responsive to the "givens" of our lives. To take life for granted in any way is to endanger that aspect of life.

Waiting. We are familiar with a kind of person who repeats to us that something important will be accomplished "after I get my promotion," "after I move to a new city," "after I recover from this death for which I am grieving." Some of us extend that to the happiness we are sure will be ours "after we die." Ultimately we realize that, for such people, no meaningful life is possible now and, therefore, will not be possible at some future time either.

Minimizing the minimal. If we ignore that which we think is too small to be of consequence for our lives, we may find ourselves at one of two extremes — either people of indecision or of hasty decision, since we have devalued that which is present to us.

When the followers of Jesus asked him how to pray, he responded with the prayer in which we pray, "Give us this day our daily bread." I believe that Jesus was talking about more than food to be eaten. He was inviting us to share our lives as well as our food. When he said of the breaking of the Bread of Life, "When you do this remember me," he was reminding us of the message of his entire life and of the many ways in which he nourished the lives of those who followed him.

Jesus, through his words and through the example of life with others from birth to death, leaves with us a clear message of the importance of the ordinary, the call to respond to each day's joys and pain. If we do not, like Jesus, strive to capture the meaning of each moment, we may mistakenly come to believe that our lives have no meaning.

Perhaps we do not often enough reflect on the meaning

hidden in the stories about the life of Jesus that are to be found in the gospels. Jesus knew well whereof he spoke when he promised "Anyone who eats this bread will live forever." This bread of renewing and revitalizing our lives. This bread of never ceasing to search for deeper and deeper meaning in our happiness and in our hurts. This bread of being attentive as we make the daily decisions which prepare us to make the larger ones. This bread of welcoming the beauty and goodness of life as it is revealed in nature. This bread of being involved in our lives as they are sometimes broken and poured out for others. This bread of embracing the mystery of life and the wonders revealed as it unfolds.

To "eat this bread" requires the kind of courage of which Robert Louis Stevenson spoke:

> The world has no room for cowards. We must be ready to toil, to suffer, to die. And yours is not less noble because no drum beats when you go out to your daily battlefields, as no crowds shout when you return from your daily victory and defeat.

3 Transpositions to a New Life

Christians have grown more familiar with the journey theme as it emerges from both the Hebrew scriptures and the gospels. We may identify with the story of Abraham who followed the call to leave his family and homeland to set out for an unknown land. We read of the excitement and misery of the Hebrew people as they sought new life with Moses as their leader. We cherish the story of Ruth who valued loyalty to her mother-in-law more than the security of her homeland. We have listened often to the familiar story of a pregnant Mary and her husband making a long and arduous journey to fulfill the demands of the state.

Mythology holds out the same journey theme in the story of Odysseus, the king of Ithaca and one of the Greek leaders in the Trojan War, as he wanders for 10 years after the fall of Troy. We are surprised by the fitfulness of a Dionysos who wandered all over the world alternately delighting people by introducing them to wine and terrifying them with the power of his armed companions.

The history of this nation is rooted in the journeys of people who craved to be free from oppression and so sought the life of promise of which they had heard. The black people who became a part of our history made the painful journey from freedom to oppression against their own will.

Writers tell us about the travels of some of our favorite imaginary people. From *Swiss Family Robinson* to Dorothy's journey with the straw man, the tin man and the lion, we can learn something about ourselves from the companionship of those who have made some unique journey that greatly changed their lives.

It is possible for a long and arduous journey to affect only the outside of a life, while the inner person remains untouched. When this happens, when someone passes through some powerful life experiences and is not affected in any significant life-giving way, we are saddened. We may speak of "unredeemed suffering," of suffering that has affected no transformation, no conversion in the life of the one from whom the journey exacted so much.

In *The Heart of Darkness*, Joseph Conrad tells the story of a man named Kurtz. It is the story of many passages, of a man challenged and outwardly transformed through grappling with a hostile environment and different cultures as he ventures into some of the darkest regions of Africa in search of ivory. His is a destructive venture into unknown regions. He does not move along the pathway of the inner journey, and is finally found by a man who recognizes that Kurtz has become less than he once was.

It's a disappointing story because the reader is introduced to the possibility of a man growing greater through a series of costly encounters. Like the story of each one of our lives, it contains the simple truth that to be alive is to have the possibility of greater life.

One thing is sure, with or without the dramatic events sketched by the writers of the great myths, history, the Bible or literature, every human person is continually growing and changing. Throughout that process there are some landmarks universally recognized and named. They represent both the changes in body and in psyche that we have come to know as infancy, childhood, adolescence and adulthood.

Some fairly recent research by behavioral scientists has taught us that the maturing of the body through these stages may or may not be accompanied by psychic maturing. Whether or not the inner process parallels the outer depends on many factors related to the physical environment, the presence or absence of favorable circumstances or of helpful role models.

To use just one example, as perplexing as the periods known as the terrible twos or stormy adolescence may be, the prospect of passing through either of these at a much later chronological age means a much more costly passage. There is something frightening about how much more difficult it would be to go through adolescence at 40 rather than during the teen years. But, whether at 14 or 40, it is a passage that must be made if we wish to live happy and healthy lives that can be shared with others.

We recognize that there are different dimensions to life's transitions. But for the purposes of discussion and reflection I separate them out and refer to inner and outer journeys and changes.

When I write about the outer journey, I wish to include decisions or events that are visible and apparent, such as the death of a loved one, separation and divorce, amputation, physical disasters that bring great destruction, economic devastation caused by the loss of a job or a business, resignation from a position or an office, and relocation.

Each of these outer changes propels us into a costly and often tumultuous inner journey where we are forced to search out hidden strengths at a time of powerlessness and insecurity. In each of these examples we enter into the often confusing, unfamiliar but intense process of grieving a loss.

People involved in such changes sometimes feel angry or frustrated because they are forced to deal with events for which they do not feel adequately prepared. They sometimes resist reality because they are torn between the self-knowledge they possess but have not yet discovered; are frightened of letting go of the certain in order to set out toward the uncertain; or are discouraged by a lack of energy when the need for endurance is great. When life brings to us some unforeseen and unwelcome, life-disrupting reality, we fluctuate between confusion and clarity, between courage and cowardice.

When we are forced to not only go on but grow on, we long to be beyond where we now are. Sensing what we must go through, we long for the end of the road.

We may resent the fact that life is not fair, and in our flailing about and resistance, we either delay or fail to set about seeking life's possibilities hidden in the present ruins. We may ignore or forget the powerful message that Jesus spoke about and enfleshed as he made his transition from Good Friday through Easter. At the beginning, the prospect of letting go may seem as costly and as consuming as the hope of catching hold of new life.

Some Obstacles Along the Way

Life's transitions, sometimes inner, sometimes outer, can be compared to transposing music to a key within the range of a performer. Some of life's possibilities may become reachable only after we have either opened ourselves or removed some of the obstacles. Life, like music, can be transposed to a key within our range.

We might ask, "Why is it so difficult to accept life's transpositions to a new and different key? Why am I so afraid of the process of discovering new life that at once increases my life's range and offers me the possibility of living more fully and more faithfully within that new and expanded range?"

St. Paul's most dramatic inner journey brought him to the place of greater life which began long before he was struck to the ground on the way to Damascus. What has sometimes been portrayed as the beginning of his conversion was rather the moment of awaking, the moment at which he began to get in touch with inner currents that had been present for a long time.

Paul's hatred of the followers of Christ was an exterior manifestation of the many unresolved questions emerging in his heart. Like ourselves, Paul carried an inner awareness of what some of the exchanges of his life would cost. When he finally let go of the obstacles that made it impossible for him to accept and embrace the way of Christians, the vigorous commitment to God's call to life emerged. With neither apology nor embarrassment, he exchanged one way for another and then set about to persuade others to do what he had done.

We strip Paul of the human condition that he shares with us if we assume that there was some magic that freed him from paying the human price for such a powerful and soul-shaking exchange of values.

In reflecting on his story, we may come to recognize some of the obstacles present in us, obstacles that interfere with an enthusiastic response to the call to life.

The expectations of others.   Because people had come to expect Paul to respond in certain ways, for him to deviate from this would arouse anger in some and suspicion in others.

If we reflect on a transition we chose with careful self-searching and constant prayer that was not well received by or accepted by people important to us, we will recognize points of identification with Paul.

The pain we experience when we realize others had carried hidden expectations that we may have violated is one of the risks involved in faithfulness to our own vision.

Practicalities.   Needs for basics like food, shelter, insurance, and support can set us asking plaguing but nonetheless practical questions about the wisdom of a decision.

Paul's pursuit of the truth that had been growing in him for longer than he realized forced him to face questions about sustaining himself as a tentmaker and his reception among his own people.

Letting go.   Paul had been a pupil of the noted Hebrew

scholar Gamaliel. His pursuit of the philosophical and religious systems of his time had claimed no small amount of his
effort and personal discipline. To allow that storehouse of
knowledge and experience to be displaced by another must
have been painful and complicated.

For us, as for Paul, the journey to some place of life that
is foreign begins with the risk of letting go.

Setting out. Lying in the dust of the road and of his past,
Paul hears a voice saying, "Get up and go into the city, and
you will be told what you are to do" (Acts 9:5). Paul sets out
on his way to the city where he meets Ananias, the man
through whom Paul recovers his sight and is filled with the
Spirit.

Because we live in a world that values activity and noise
more than solitude and silence, we may not understand the
life sounds deep inside us which could give direction to our
lives if we would invest in the disciplined process of discovering and then listening to these messages.

Keeping on.   The dusty road to Damascus was but a con-
tinuation of a life journey that had its beginnings in Paul's following the sacred traditions of the Hebrew reliance on Yahweh's promise of life. His trust in the messages of life he
received through Gamaliel and others was now an investment
in his ability to trust the way of life to which Jesus called those
who wished to learn.

Any serious and disciplined investment that we make at
any point along our journey can bear fruit for us, as for Paul,
when the direction of our life is changed.

Arriving somewhere without noticing where we have been. Paul's
call to change the direction of his life was not an invitation to
abandon his past or to deny it. Rather it was a call to search
for the connections that existed between what had been and
what would be. To be a growing human being necessitates
that we carry our past with us, that we stay awake in the
present and that we give shape and direction to our dreams
for the future.

Paul claimed that he wrote and preached out of the strengths of three dimensions of his life, three separate sets of influences — Roman roots, Hebrew traditions and now Christian convictions according to which he chose to live. Through prayer and self-reflection we remember our past, respond faithfully to our present, and grow into the future.

Sometimes the changes in the inner life of someone who has made a painful passage are not immediately visible. But, in time both that person and those who know him well may realize that great change has taken place.

Failing to cherish the journey. When Paul picked himself up from the ground and through the guidance of others made his way to Damascus, observers who recognized this fiery opponent of the Christian way must have wondered at his seeming docility. It is not likely that this segment of Paul's inner journey was one of comfortable confidence. Even when Paul began to proclaim the message of his newly chosen way, he must have been aware of onlookers who could not trust what they were hearing from the lips of this former enemy.

When we have passed through some turning point, we gradually let go of the initial discomfort and then eventually feel at home in our newly discovered place of life. Usually it is only in retrospect, when we have had time to remember where we have been and have savored the life that is now possible, do we move from following with reluctant steps to accepting and then to cherishing where we now are.

Can We Develop a Receptivity to Life Transitions?

A woman who has been somewhat of a role model for me had just left the hospital after a mysterious physical condition. She associated her illness with leaving a job she had held for more than 25 years and her struggle with her new position.

Our lives had been quite different in that respect. While she had a lengthy stay in one place, I had a number of moves and transitions. We both knew that these changes had not always been easy, but from them I gained confidence in new beginnings. For my friend it was the lack of change that had been painful.

As we discussed our lives, she shared her fears and described the varying forms that her suffering had taken. She looked at me and with a tone of regret and a look of sadness said, "I stayed too long. I wish I had not given myself so many reasons for staying when something inside told me that I should move on."

She was not able to allow change in her life and was not able to transform the painful endings into a confidence in new beginnings. Whether the decision to move on is ours or is made by someone else, the letting go and moving on will carry with it the pain of loss, pain somehow related to how much of ourselves we have given to what we are now leaving.

We may resist making that transposition to "this difficult and unaccustomed key" even though we have some hints that we will have more room for life. This is the kind of unsung heroism of which T.S. Eliot speaks in *The Cocktail Party:*

> There is another way, if you have the courage . . . You will journey blind. But the way leads towards possession of what you have sought for in the wrong place.

Each well-made decision strengthens us for the journey through the next one. Each place of new life allows us to look back with gratitude for our perseverance that has brought us to some greater sense of self, some larger world in which to grow.

Though I had not known this, I recognized that I had also been an example to this suffering woman and that she wished to emulate my courage in continually sensing some new place of life, some new way of sharing whatever gifts I have.

I know that I have found such strong meaning through

hearing or reading about the lives of others as they described the price they had paid for caring enough about themselves to enter into unknown lands (sometimes literally) and to deal with whatever insecurities they may have had. We do carry on with an eye that notices and an ear that listens and makes it possible for us to say, "If you could do it, so can I."

While making good decisions with a generous measure of self-reflection and personal assessment we must make a commitment to remember that no single decision can destroy us and that we can find our way again through another decision. Sometimes it is not possible to follow the words of John F. Kennedy when he said, "Not only must we make good decisions, but we must make our decisions good." The realization that some decision has not led us to greater life is disappointing and may be disruptive of our lives and the lives of others.

We are blessed, once again, in sometimes having role models for this part of the journey that appear now to be a sidetrack or a dead end as we regroup and say to ourselves, "I can and will choose life again and again." A God who loves us proclaims clearly, "I am offering you life or death, blessing or curse. Choose life, then, so that you and your descendants may live" (Dt 30:19).

The Practicalities of the Process

When we are in the process of decision-making that will change our lives in some profound ways, we experience ourselves in some new ways. Our awareness of both our strengths and limitations is heightened. Fears arise out of the realization that C.S. Lewis was right when he said "One who has journeyed in a strange land cannot return unchanged." We have an instinctive sense that tells us that we will lose some part of who we have been in exchange for something unknown and feared even if more beautiful than what was lost.

Selecting a person with whom to take counsel as we face some transition is as important as it may be difficult. The presence of a person who can help us evaluate our strengths and limitations, who can help us discover the essential questions, is very important. We may need a second presence who will not make our decision or manipulate us in the direction they have already chosen. A person who will be there for us, offering unconditional acceptance while also challenging us, is like the tough and tender love of God.

Once we are in the process of transition, there are no clearly defined signposts. It's an area of unexplored life since no two persons have the same history or sets of circumstances. After all the personal assessment, discussion with others, prayer, faith and love, at some point we must decide and then, like the figure in Ezekiel 47:1-7, walk into the water. We cannot wade in just ankle deep or knee deep. The important decisions of life require that we keep going and trust that the swirling waters will not destroy us.

The only life that each of us has and is responsible for is our own. Whether we are young or old, married or single, believers or unbelievers, the personal journey underlies any journey that we seek to make with others. The love of others can nourish us, strengthen us, reinforce our belief in ourselves, but the inner journey and the outer journey that is uniquely ours cannot be either given over or taken over by another. We walk as separate selves first and then as companions who share the journey that each makes.

We cannot be subject to the decision that others would make for us, for another cannot walk this journey for us. As Bernard Lonergan said in his *Collection*, "There is a critical point in the development of a person, when a person realizes that his decisions affect him more deeply than they effect events outside of himself." He believes that this critical point is reached when a person finally realizes that it is up to each of us to decide who we shall become and what direction we wish to give to our lives. At this point, the matter is no longer simple decision making; it has become a matter of personal integrity.

Why Does It Have to Hurt So Much?

If we seek to speak of major life transitions in merely poetic or philosophical terms, we shall have missed both the meaning and the message. My memories of my life and the insights I have gained when others have told me of the price they paid for dramatic changes in their journeys evoke feelings of doubt and terror, of insecurity and anger. We begin to doubt ourselves as we are viewed quizzically by some and know that we may lose the respect of others. Few of us can claim to have run with arms open into the darkness. We are much more aware of the light we regret leaving.

Thrust into this fearsome place through a faithful response to life's call does not change the dread, nor does it relieve the intensity of the pain of loss.

We cannot rely on the false hope that it will hurt less than we expect nor can we hope to shorten the time of pain. Our very faithfulness to where we are and to what we are presently involved in makes leaving, setting out, and moving on such a costly leap toward life.

Others may tell us of their newfound life after some form of dying. They may describe to us the new energy that gave them a sense of exhilaration. They may share their newfound strength and gifts but they cannot give us that life, transfuse that energy, or bestow those gifts on us.

Psychologists tell us that good decisions well made are sources of energy. Decisions once made are no longer places into which energy is being poured. But, it is usually only later, after we have walked through some difficult miles, that we are able to look back over our shoulder and see how far we have come. It is only later that we know that we did more than just survive.

If the road we presently walk is not one that offers the

best possibilities for life, if there are inner roads that we have
avoided, then the price we will pay is certainly not too great to
go in search of a better way.

    There is another way, if we have the courage. . . .

    . . . the first I could describe in familiar
terms because you have seen it, as we
have all seen it,
Illustrated, more or less, in the lives
of those about us.
The second is unknown, and so requires faith—
The kind of faith that issues from despair . . .
You will journey blind.

                    The Cocktail Party, T. S. Eliot

4 Pursuing Life-Giving Questions

He had all the wrong dreams. All wrong. He never
knew who he was.
Death of a Salesman, Arthur Miller

There is a universal tendency in human beings to look for
ready-made answers. Because we are sometimes insecure and
lack confidence in our ability to make good decisions, we often rely more on the experiences of others than we do on our
own. Because we are afraid of making mistakes, we look for
some authority to show us the way or give us a formula.

Even those of us who pride ourselves on our self-
assurance and independence do sometimes gravitate toward
that person or source of information that claims certainty.
Most of all, we are afraid of hurting those we care about and
so we hope to discover some clearly defined way of sharing
friendship, a way that offers us the hope that we will not fail.

We are all, sometimes, answer-seekers. Our fear of the
unknown produces in us a kind of paralysis which we believe
will be relieved once we have found a clearly defined direction
or a well-formulated dream.

To invest our energy in the quest for an answer, a formula, a fail-safe blueprint for living is to search for life where
it can never be found. To rely primarily on a set of unchanging norms is to risk the inner death that will surely result from
an unchanging life. To seek such security is to look for life in
the wrong places. It is like setting out for a city of unknown
location using the wrong map.

Because we manifest this lack of certainty, other people will try to make protecting us their prerogative and set themselves up as authorities for our lives.

Parents and teachers, who may appropriately serve as guides through our younger years when we are testing our own values and questioning our life direction, sometimes fail to allow us some margin for trial and error, sometimes fail to set us free. Their overprotective attitudes may rob us of important opportunities to grow up.

Institutions and governments too often offer the message that they are better authorities on the lives of individuals than people themselves are. Efforts to control the lives of others rather than providing an environment in which life can develop sometimes makes it difficult for people to develop a sense of responsibility appropriate to their years.

No single authority, no complete set of answers, no clearly defined way is applicable to the lives of all. While others can help us evaluate, lead us to insight, challenge us to try again, and offer us their acceptance and support, they cannot decide for us. There are no clearly defined answers for most of life's ever-changing questions. And all too often we even begin with the wrong questions.

Those in the helping professions are well aware of this preoccupation with answers, and of the expectation that there is a mistake-proof way. They know that people wish to avoid the pain of both uncertainty and error.

It is not uncommon for parents who have a drug-abusing teenager to look for someone who can provide a clearly marked course resulting in immediate and total recovery.

People involved in troubled marriages want someone else to decide whether or not the marriage is still viable. Instead of seeking insight into the relationship and being patient with themselves, they want to be immediately free of their discomfort.

Divorced, remarried Catholics often want a simple and clear "yes" or "no" answer to their question about the reception of the Eucharist. They expect someone else to free them of their responsibility to evaluate their relationship with God and the church.

People experiencing physical pain that does not fit the predicted courses of treatment often demand an impossibly clear analysis from a doctor, one that will unfailingly result in total and nearly instant freedom from pain.

As a teacher, I was exhilarated by the student who entered into the process of learning with interest and openness. And I was distressed when significant numbers of students wanted only to be given an answer.

Today some false prophets destroy the possibility of life for their followers by demanding faithfulness to unquestioned precepts and interfere with the process of mature conscience formation. These self-proclaimed prophets preach a gospel that does not give witness to the goodness of human life with its resilience and spontaneity.

The life of Jesus gives adequate witness to the truth that while there are ideals and values by which we are invited to live, there are no clearly defined means by which to do this. We have his invitation to be among the pilgrim people who through listening to his questions of life as well as to his life, will not avoid pain, but will grow through and beyond it.

We should not devalue the experience and expertise of others. The teacher, the minister, the counsellor, the doctor, the priest, the drug rehabilitator, and many others have learned what we may not yet know.

Educational systems, churches, governments and all of the various disciplines enrich and widen our inner worlds. In each resides some valuable body of truth and some wisdom accumulated over centuries.

But, a God who loves us and created us with searching hearts and questioning minds calls us to be faithful to these two gifts. Out of the sometimes annoying questions and through the gnawing uncertainties of life we are stretched and invited to grow.

The quest for ready-made answers is reflective of the knights who set out in search of the holy grail, of the explorers who believed that there was a fountain of youth, and of the ancient alchemists who believed that a certain combination of mysterious chemical elements would produce the elixir of life. These stories reveal frustration and disappointment because of the futility of their adventures. They are a reminder of long years of involvement with projects that had no possibility of dreams fulfilled, or of expended energy rewarded and renewed. Such stories provide us with useful insights and provide us the opportunity to recognize the fruitlessness of unrealistic dreams.

Where Shall We Discover the Truth of Life?

When we rely on the strength that comes from inside and test our experience against that of others; when we weigh our gifts and our limitations carefully; when we evaluate the risk as well as the possibilities of the dream, then we take responsibility for the direction of our lives. When we ask questions that do not have either quick or easy answers, we begin to free ourselves of the crippling effects of expecting or demanding answers.

We cannot shape personal dreams if we live out of someone else's dream which we falsely perceive as a blueprint for our lives. Loss of creativity, of vision and, ultimately, of the fullest life that could be ours results when we look outside ourselves for certainty, when we ignore the rich possibilities that our experience could reveal to us.

Dag Hammarskjold once said that "There is no formula to teach us how to arrive at maturity and there is no grammar for the language of the inner life."

Facing decisions often forces us to return to our own inner resources and to test these against what we see and hear from others. We need imagination and some tested experiences in order to trust the insights that we have and the objective reality we perceive. In this context, we will be more likely to formulate our own questions, questions that will set us upon a road that ready-made answers would never lead us.

The starting place is found in seeking and shaping the life-giving questions — framing questions that are powerful enough to unlock our best energies. Just as there is no all-inclusive handbook that contains the answers asked by those in pursuit of life, so there is no place to find preformulated questions suited to each of our lives. Even the questions we arrive at with great difficulty during a specific phase of our lives are not likely to be useful at another time.

As we grow and change, and the lives of those with whom we share life change, so does the culture in which we are immersed undergo its breakdowns and breakthroughs. The finest institutions, families, and nations are not static. A seemingly unnoticed change in one may greatly affect another.

Whence comes the truth of life? If it begins with abandoning the insatiable thirst for answers, it does not end with the discovery of a lengthy set of questions. The questions must be life-giving and not stagnant; they must be open-ended, continually replaced and/or reformulated.

We need to nourish our best creative energies so that we might translate our life experiences into questions out of which new and richer life experiences can emerge. That involves the painful process of growing up and away from our reliance on those who would, by the imposition of answers and/or injunctions, limit our freedom to choose our own direction after assessing our values and our hidden strengths.

Contrasting Some Lifeless and Some Life-Giving Questions

The differences between lifeless and life-giving questions

may not be so apparent. The identification of each may lead us to a process of self-reflection in which we rely, to some extent, on the resources that are to be found in reflecting on our past.

Rethinking a particular event may open for us the possibility of recreating what happened in such a way as to gain insight into our present which demands that same attention.

Sometimes we may consider a certain situation or decision that lies ahead in such a way that we project our thoughts and walk through the possibilities beforehand. While avoiding conclusions, such an exercise may nourish our creative energies and prepare us better for the event or decision when it is immediate.

A question like, "What would I do if?" is not useless imagining; nor is it necessarily predictive of exactly what we might choose. But it does get us involved with something that is important to us before it happens and so it prepares us to deal with it better when the time comes.

The question, "What would seem to be an ideal response in terms of my own dreams for the future?" helps clarify our goals and our sense of the path we are on, allowing us to alter our direction or to recommit ourselves to the present one.

Exploring Some Questions

I would like to further clarify the difference between life-less and life-giving questions, and have separated the following into questions related to personal growth, to offering friendship, to dealing with broken relationships, and to our relationship with God.

Questions related to self-discovery and self-cherishing

I will begin with personal growth because I believe that relationship to self is basic to loving others and God. The two great commandments, with their injunction to love God above all else and to love my neighbor as myself, tell me that unless I am investing well in discovering and giving direction to who I am, I will have nearly insurmountable obstacles to loving others and allowing them to love me. This may include my refusal to accept even God's love.

The question is not . . .	**The question is . . .**
Do others love me?	Do I love myself?
Do I have the gifts and strength that I need for my life?	Am I seeking to discover my gifts and my strengths?
Am I lovable?	Am I trying to discover what it means to love?
How can I avoid failing?	How do I deal with failure?
How can I avoid all risks?	How do I decide which risks may be a source of life for me?
Do I have all the information that I need to be sure in making this decision?	Have I sought enough information so that I can act responsibly?
What if someone else does not approve of a decision that I believe I must make?	Do I have confidence that this decision is faithful to my life?
Is it good to be human?	Do I accept and cherish my humanness with all that this implies?

The threefold nature of human life — my relationship with myself, with others and with God — invites me to pursue the questions that will lead me to discover, cherish, and share who I am, believing that a God who created me stays with me and surrounds me with nourishing love. Any question I ask that prepares me to accept this truth is a life-giving question. Any question that sidetracks this basic truth will not lead me to a place of greater life.

Questions related to offering and receiving the gift of friendship

There is no more important pursuit for human life than sharing our lives with others in ways that are faithful to both who we are and who our friends are. Faithfulness to this shared quest for life is at the heart of who I am and who I can become rather than what I may or may not be able to do. Faithfulness to sharing life with others in relationships that are life-giving for both helps us discover the meaning in what we do.

The question is not . . .	The question is . . .
How can I be a person always ready to give?	How can I be a person who is equally comfortable with giving and receiving?
Have I loved another too much?	How well have I loved?
Will someone I have hurt forgive me?	Can I forgive myself when I have hurt another?
Will I make mistakes in this relationship?	Am I honest in my efforts to love this person?
How have others failed me?	Am I failing myself and, therefore, failing friends?
Can I trust another person?	Do I trust myself?
Why do I love so imperfectly?	How can I accept the fact that all human loving is imperfect?
How can I hide my feelings from another?	How can I share my feelings with someone I say I care about?
How can we avoid fighting?	What does it mean to be fair when we do face conflict?

Friendships are sometimes destroyed by our careless inattentiveness to our feelings and our lack of respect for the feelings of another. Sometimes we act out of sets of half-truths which we have unknowingly internalized. Some of these which affect the nature of our way of being friend are: "It is better to give than to receive" while the whole truth is that unless we can both give and receive we have not provided for the gifts of a friend. We say that we want to be "selfless" in relationships, but, unless my self is totally involved and present to an important relationship it cannot be a place of life. Seeking to be "altruistic," to love without expectation of return, can lead us to either ignore or fail to identify and then share the honest expectations and needs that we have in every relationship. Sometimes instead of giving ourselves to a relationship, we give ourselves away through some hidden need and so we begin the destruction of a friendship.

Questions related to broken relationships

Because we fail to notice the erosion factors in a friendship, because we sometimes do not question our small failures to be present to ourselves or others, relationships are broken. Our faithfulness to life and the fact that good friendships are at the center of our existence makes broken relationships intensely painful.

In grieving the loss of a friend who was an important channel of life for us, we flail about in unpredicted and unpredictable emotional responses which frighten us and drain us of energy.

Whether or not our grieving enables us to cope with the loss while also moving us to openness to new life depends on the responses we make. Our course may be set almost completely by the inner questions we pose.

The question is not . . .	The question is . . .
Why has this friend failed me?	How have I failed myself?
What was someone else's part in this destruction?	What was my part in the loss of this relationship?
Why must I grieve this loss?	How am I grieving?
Why must it hurt so much?	Will this pain lead me to better future relationships?

Where was God when this relationship was being destroyed?	Where was I when this destructiveness was going on?
Will I find another friend?	When am I ready to again enter into relationship?
How can I be sure that I will never be hurt by someone again?	Will I hurt myself again through my failure to learn from this broken friendship?
How could this have happened so suddenly?	Why did I fail to notice the signs that were there all along?

Often in broken friendships we are forced to deal with our blindness to our ways of being a friend or our failure to be sufficiently present to ourselves. Two people set the patterns in a relationship and our future life depends on our discovering our part. We search the ruins not to punish ourselves but to discover the keys to life and to more loving bonds. We acknowledge the fact that the only life we have charge of and can give direction to is our own.

Questions related to God

When I listen carefully to the questions I am often asked about God, I am aware that people also reveal their images of God. Freeing people of deeply set images of God and the expectations they carry is a reminder of the strong desire that exists in the hearts of believing Christians to be faithful to their lives. The shackles binding them to misinformation about God seem to be among the strongest.

The question is not . . .	**The question is . . .**
Will God punish me for this?	Why have I chosen to punish myself in this way?
Will God forgive me for this?	Can I forgive myself?
If I do this, will God send me to hell?	If I do this, what kind of person will I become?

Will God accept my human limitations?

Have I come to terms with all the aspects of what being human means?

The bible says that if I ask God for this in prayer, it will be given. Why didn't God keep that promise?

What is the nature of prayer? What happens to my relationship with God when I pray?

What will life be like in heaven?

How am I living now?

The Source of Life-Giving Questions

Shaping questions that are for life result in part from gaining insight and wisdom in the process of living. Sometimes it takes a dramatic interaction with life, either happy or sad, to heighten our awareness of where life for us is to be found. Sometimes we stumble onto insights without necessarily being able to trace their origin. Sometimes being in the presence of a person who goes to the heart of the matter triggers our ability to do the same.

When I think of forming questions which prepare us to recognize or discover some new facet of life, I am reminded of an old woman potter and the wisdom she was willing to share.

A friend wanted to take a series of slides that would show the making of a stoneware pot. We drove down every side road on Cape Cod that either led us to some town or that had been marked with a simple sign that read "Potter" and had an arrow indicating the direction we should take. After repeated fruitless ventures, we found ourselves at the tip of the Cape in Provincetown. We then had the good fortune to stop a man who was able to direct us to the potter's shed in which we found a woman of more than 70 years.

She took great pride in showing us some of her work and was happy to turn a pot for us. After she had worked the clay and prepared it for the wheel, she sat down and gave us a single direction: "Please take pictures that show only my hands and the wheel."

As she worked the clay and turned the wheel, she made a number of statements for which she offered no further description, but statements which revealed some profound truths.

She began by saying, "The condition of the clay matters. Even though you can select different kinds of clay for different purposes, you have to prepare them for the wheel . . . Yes, the condition of the clay matters."

She went on, "A part of the process is unpredictable. So, no two results are ever exactly the same. It's like life, you can make decisions but you can never predict the exact outcome."

I noticed the strong hands and arms of this woman, gentle in voice and manner, sturdy in appearance and inner spirit. She described the pliability of the clay and her belief that there was a direct relationship between its pliability and its strength. Then she added, almost as an aside, "If you can't bend a little and give some, life will eventually break you. It's just the way it is, you know."

As the wheel continued to respond to the action of her foot and knee, I saw how carefully she positioned herself so that one of her hands could work from the inside, placing pressure on the clay, and the other hand could work from the outside of the gradually forming pot. There were two sets of opposing forces in the two hands.

Once again, the woman spoke to us about life. "I have to remember to notice what both of my hands are doing. If I put more pressure on the one outside the pot, I can cause it to collapse. If I apply too much from the inside, it will bulge outward."

This time, it was my turn to make the association and the woman smiled when I said, "I used to think that pots were shaped from the inside and I used to liken that to the inner values that are the most important for the shaping of our lives."

The woman potter did not allow me to finish when she interrupted to say, "You are wrong, my friend. Life, like the pot I am turning, is shaped by two sets of opposing forces. There are forces inside of us and there are forces that come to us from the outside, like our family and friends, or the country in which we live."

And her final words just before she removed the pot from the wheel summarized not only the making of a pot but her basic belief about life:

> Both my hands shaped this pot. And, the place where it actually forms is a place of tension between the pressure applied from the outside and the pressure of the hand on the inside. That's the way my life has been. Sadness and death and misfortune and the love of friends and all the things that happened to me that I didn't even choose. All of that influenced my life. But, there are things I believe in about myself, my faith in God and the love of some friends that worked on the insides of me. My life, like this pot, is the result of what happened on the outside and what was going on inside of me. Life, like this pot, comes to be in places of tension. Life comes to be when we learn how to avoid looking for answers and finally learn how to ask the questions that will bring us to life.

There is a tendency in us to want to live tension-free. But, like the woman potter, I believe that this tension is God's gift to us, a gift that sometimes will not permit us to escape its presence. I believe that our creative energies are activated by just that kind of upsetting tension. It is in responding to this gnawing discomfort that we have the possibility of giving shape to dreams that are at once faithful to who we are and who we can become.

5 False Gods Before Us

You shall have no strange gods, shall worship no alien god.

Psalm 81:9

In the retreats that I have had the opportunity to conduct in recent years, one important and somewhat surprising question has been raised in all the groups: "Who is your God?"

It had reminded me that as a child in a Catholic grade school, I memorized the Ten Commandments, and with a little effort, I can still conjure up some of the sketches in the catechism. Remembering the picture of Moses coming down the mountain to find God's chosen followers worshipping a golden calf, I knew as a child that the first commandment would be no problem for me. I felt confident that no image of any animal, gold or otherwise, would ever replace the God of my "God bless Mommy and Daddy," or my "Thank you, God, for the new book Daddy bought me."

It has taken many years of living and intense self-evaluation, as well as the words of teachers and retreat directors, to recognize that the first commandment, "I am the Lord, your God, you shall not set strange gods before me," relates to my life. It has been and sometimes is a problem for me. Golden calves come in various shapes, sizes and compositions. I have also learned that I am not alone in my sometimes unidentified ability to put God aside for other powers in my life.

Sometimes we create a god who is not God out of our

fears, insecurities, and even our enemies. We create the image and then pray to a god that we hope to manipulate by our words, a god that we expect to free us from suffering, keeping us forever warm and comfortably safe from harm. We seek refuge in a god that will protect us from mistakes, thus keeping us children. We claim allegiance to a god that cuts us off when we sin, rejects us when we fail, and tolerates only those who are already perfect.

We raise questions that have nothing to do with God and little to do with our own lives and then we wait for answers that will set us on a clearly defined path to easily attainable life.

We have set certain authority figures in God's place, looking for them to do what we must do for ourselves, expecting them to show us once and for all the way to life. We are willing to put our lives in their hands, as if they were God, because we are not confident enough of who God is.

In God's name we say we are afraid of making mistakes in loving while failing to notice that our fears keep us from loving at all. We become people of indecision, never embracing life with open arms.

We have not taken seriously enough the crippling effects of having allowed our image of God to be defaced even when we do this in God's name.

Sometimes we are afraid to allow God to love us out of some instinctive but hidden fear that if we let God's love in, then faithfulness to that love may lead us to deeper commitment and greater faithfulness to our own lives and to a realization that there is more to our lives than just ourselves.

Sometimes churches, instead of providing an environment in which people can explore the truth of God's ever-revealing presence, become only places of discipline and judgment. Rather than being reassured that God's love can be ignored but never lost, people hear messages of a God of conditional love and selectivity, of a God accepting some and rejecting others.

Sometimes we pursue distorted images of a god who behaves as humans do rather than seeking the God who cannot be confined to the limited behavior of human nature. Because we fear extending our reach to a God beyond our imagining and our experience, we seek to confine the creator to the limitations of the created. The false gods before us are as numerous as our fears and failures. The false gods have only the powers over us that we have, often without knowing it, given to them.

It Makes a Difference Who Your God Is

I believe that, by our nature, we are religious beings. I believe that at the center of our existence is an instinctive quest for association with, and reliance on, a presence greater than we are. To be fully human means to continually seek a greater awareness of, understanding of, and response to that being in whom we are centered by the very fact of our having been created.

Religion, which is rooted in the Latin word meaning "to bind together," is the binding force in human life. This force has the possibility of guiding us to what is most fully human and, therefore, most faithful to the creator's plan for us. This force has the possibility of leading us most deeply into ourselves and calling us to reach out from that center beyond the confines of our own lives into the lives of others.

Whether or not religion is a binding force or an enslaving place depends on who our god is. It depends on who or what power most influences our lives.

The success of Alcoholics Anonymous begins with the first step of acknowledging that someone or something has power over a human life that can only be broken by recognizing that this power is destructive of life. Alcoholics Anonymous then challenges people to reclaim their lives and to give them over to a God of life and not of destruction. The program holds no promise that this is an easy task, for the search for the God of life is never-ending and often painful. After attending a retreat weekend, a recovering alcoholic wrote in a card, "Recovery is a path . . . not a sudden landing." So, the quest for the God of life, the God that binds life and lives together, is not a single event or decision but a journey that is never completed. The God of life cares too much for each of us to offer a life that can be cheaply obtained.

We can claim to be religious women and men only if we have sought some binding force for life, some common glue that identifies us with one another and with the source of life. We can claim to be religious women and men only if we see the struggle to deal with and accept our humanness as necessarily and intimately connected to our pursuit of the discovery of, and our belief in, the power that is the God of life. We are religious women and men only if our life has a threefold dimension, and includes an investment in living this threefold injunction to love God and our neighbor as ourselves.

Accepting God's existence and the importance of this step toward human life is no easy venture. This acceptance will affect the way we live and will exact a higher price for the life we desire. As Morris West says in *The Clowns of God:*

> Once you accept the existence of God — however you define him, however you explain your relationship to Him — then you are caught forever with his presence in the center of all things. You are also caught with the fact that man is a creature who walks in two worlds and traces upon the walls of his cave the wonders and the nightmare experiences of his spiritual pilgrimage.

Ironically, the decision to follow a false god is not less costly or intense. We are often too easily tricked into believing that the pearl of great price can be easily obtained, that there is a bargain counter where things of great value are nearly given away.

Witness the tragedy of cults in which people who are often confused and set adrift are enslaved to false promises of instant community and security. Good people who are hurting or simply weary with life's injustices and inequalities follow, without question, those who profess to know exactly where life is for them.

Who of us can forget the horrors of a Jonestown where entire families followed a command to take their own lives because they had committed themselves to following a man who had set himself up as an all-knowing god. A man who encouraged people to escape from life to a place where they were promised not that they would find richer life but simply that they would be free of its pressures. In subjecting themselves to this form of enslavement, adults were changed into terminal children and the lives of their children were never allowed to unfold.

Some reflection on the phenomena of cults can awaken us to the destructiveness that inevitably follows when, in our desire to avoid pain, we short-circuit all possibilities for life. Some thought given to the harm that is done whenever we look to someone else for answers and for a pain-free way to life reveals the intensity of the implications related to a built-in human need for some binding force — which is religion — and some centering place — which is God.

Who Has Formed Our Images of God?

To survive our own infancy, we need people around us who care enough to let us know that fingers meeting electrical sockets, hot stoves and sharp instruments is not good.

To learn to read and spell, we rely on the assistance of teachers who understand what is involved in the process and who guide us through it with care.

To learn to pray we need parents who are praying people and who take time to teach us to tell God what we think we need and to thank God for the many things we have been

given. We need someone whose life is a role model for the
meaning of the words "please" and "thank you."

We rely on others whose education, experience and wisdom can help us to learn or to find our way. We ask questions
of those who have facts that are yet unfamiliar to us. We walk
for a time in the footsteps of those who have explored the way
before us. But there is a point when we begin to recognize our
need to rely on our own learning, whatever wisdom we have
acquired, and whatever piece of the road we have travelled.
We risk the possibility of judgment not yet mature and paths
too limited for the decision at hand. We need the understanding and support of those who set us free to discover our way.

At this crucial time key people either facilitate life for us
or hinder it. They help make it possible for us to become religious men and women following the truth or formula-
followers who seek answers for life rather than a way to life.
They are people who are in a position to offer us the unconditional acceptance that prepares us to believe in the unconditional love of a God.

Unfortunately, sometimes these and other people carry
within them, without their knowing it, images of God that are
not faithful to who God is. They sometimes believe that religion is more of a set of roadblocks rather than a binding force
that links us to one another and frees us for life. They are
sometimes people who live out of some fundamental belief
that "security first" is the message of the gospel and that risking for life is not faithful.

Lillian Hellman has an almost too powerful description
in *Pentimento* of the harm she believes is done, perhaps unwit-
tingly, as children receive an inner heritage from their parents
and from others in a position to influence and shape their life
direction. She says:

> . . . God help all children as they move into a time of
> life they do not understand and must struggle through

the precepts they have picked from the garbage cans of older people, clinging with the passion of the lost to the odds and ends that will mess them up for all time, or hating the trash so much they will have to waste their future on the hatred.

Some of us are more vulnerable than others to the influence of those who set walls around us in the name of caring. Some of us are more susceptible than others to the undue influence of those in positions of authority and those who put themselves into the role of self-appointed gods.

Some people are, by their nature, more questioning than others and are more reluctant to catch hold of the over-abundant supply of answers for life that are too readily available.

But, whatever the influences and the input, the truth is that many people, when the time arrives that they are looked upon as mature adults, have been greatly influenced by those whose notions of who God is are inaccurate and destructive of any basis for belief.

Believing men and women must carefully avoid being put into the position of being "god" for someone who is afraid to take personal responsibility for life — someone who wants an answer, a road map for making the journey through difficult decision or transition times.

Some Common False Gods Before Us

For whatever reasons, the end result of these external forces and internal limitations is that we may live out our lives responding to any one of the following inaccurate images of God.

The punishing god. When asked what word comes to mind when they think about God, many people respond with the word "punishment." They are not able to explain from where or from whom they first heard about this god, but they

do speak of how greatly it influences their lives. It is not that
they believe that this is just one aspect of the nature of the god
about whom they have heard, it has become their overriding
inner stance. Out of such an inner attitude it is not likely that
the threefold nature of life will unfold. Fear of punishment is
healthy when the fear is proportionate or related to something
which may deserve punishment. But the fear of which we
speak goes far beyond this.

The unforgiving god.   In 1917, Karl Barth, a Lutheran
theologian, spoke about this false god as a "therefore god" who
allows no margin for error, no second chances. He suggested
that if Christians are to be faithful to the life to which God
calls, they will not succeed in this effort unless and until they
replace this "therefore god" with a "nevertheless god" whose
forgiveness is always there for us. Perhaps the best image of a
nevertheless presence is the father in the story of the prodigal
son who returns home after he has squandered his inheritance, and who is received without question.

The manipulative god.   Some people do not believe in the
concept of Christian freedom as a given for life. They live out
of the notion that they are the victims of the circumstances
dealt by a god who gets people to do what he wants by controlling what happens in their lives. Any person who does not
believe that human freedom is given from the hands of a loving God is not likely to respond with openness to their life experiences.

The manipulatable god.   A woman whose husband had
died of cancer told me that she was through with God and
prayer. She said that when she learned of her husband's illness, she and her children began to pray together every day.
"And," she said, "after all those prayers, he still died. What use
is prayer? What good is a god who is not faithful?" A man told
me, "My wife is an alcoholic. I prayed and God has neither
changed my wife nor gotten her into treatment."

These incidents reflect both a misunderstanding of who

God is and what prayer is. The main influence of prayer is that it has the possibility of changing the one who prays. A God who loves all and respects the freedom of each will not be manipulated by either our prayers or our good works.

The impatient god. Human beings learn, grow and change slowly. Sometimes life seems like a process of taking two steps backward and one forward. We repeat past errors. We do not sense or believe in our growth. We are apt to say, as one woman said to me, "There is no point in trying anymore. I have made so many mistakes. God isn't going to wait forever for me."

She is wrong. She has projected her own impatience with herself onto God. She also needs to free herself of the image of God that she carries.

The god who rejects the human condition. Many human beings do not really like and perhaps do not even accept their humanness. Being human is messy. It includes some failure, some insecurities, some weakness, some sinfulness. Because of this we sometimes forget that we have gifts, some known but many undiscovered. Most good people do not like themselves enough.

We have taken the gift of our humanness and refused to believe that it is a sign of God's great love for us. We have even looked upon it as though we were either sentenced or condemned to be human.

The best reminder of the creator's love for us came in the form of Jesus, God's own son. "Like us," says St. Paul, "in all things save sin."

If we spend our lives doing battle against that which we most are — namely, human — then we will never discover our gifts and will not cherish the gift that we are.

The whimsical god. Because life and our response to it is often unpredictable, we falsely conclude that we are the victims of a fitful god, a whimsical god, who does not take us seriously — a god who does not hold us tenderly and surely, but rather a god whose responses are dependent on nothing we can perceive as substantial or faithful.

But our God is faithful beyond our imagining, reliable beyond any human experience. God's is a presence that is not passing, a strength to sustain and support us when we find faithfulness difficult.

The god of dualism.   Some of the heritage of the ancient Greeks has flowed over into and been passed on in Christian teaching. Their belief that spirit is good and matter evil has invaded our belief.

Scripture scholars and theologians have been doing battle with this heresy for centuries but they have not yet freed us of its influences. Part of this error interferes with our taking responsibility for our lives.

Someone has said that too many Christians live with their heads in the heavens and their feet planted nowhere. This has allowed us to devalue not only what we do here on earth, but even who we are. We live with an "after I get to heaven" mentality that ignores the importance of a life here, and leads us to invest little of ourselves in relationships with others, self or God.

The book of Genesis tells us that, after each day of creation, God looked at what was created and "God saw that it was good."

William Ellery Channing, who lived at the turn of the 18th century, said:

> We do not honor God by breaking down the human soul, connecting it with him only by a tie of slavish dependence. It is God's glory that he creates beings like himself, free beings . . . that he confers on them the reality of life and not the show of power.

Sometimes I am afraid that people may not live long enough to shed their false gods or that they may not have an experience of something that can break through what is false and force them to discover the truth of who God is. Sometimes the truth of life and the belief in the goodness of a loving God only become part of our lives when some tragedy necessitates our entering into our own lives more deeply and shedding our destructive baggage.

Countless people suffer greatly because they have given their lives over to a powerful and controlling god. The images they carry are not easily shed. Sometimes they are like shackles which can only be removed with the help of another.

Sometimes people are afraid they are losing their faith if they question the God of their childhood or reject the accumulation of inherited injunctions. I believe that Socrates' statement, "The unexamined life is not worth living," is also true of faith and religion. A faith that defies questioning and an image of God that cannot be thoroughly examined are not life-giving. The questions at the center of who we are and who God is emanate from a religion that binds life and lives together.

Other Gods of Power

Other gods outside of us have power over us — gods chosen by us that powerfully influence the kind of persons we become. Each is destructive. Each has the possibility of becoming an all-encompassing influence on all the dimensions of our lives.

A god named power. There is a difference between having power and making its pursuit the driving force in our lives. There is a difference between the power that is born of genuine respect for ability and that which is sought because we are unsure of our abilities.

The destructiveness of power arises not from its presence but in its becoming central to our lives. The ability to use power for life, our own and that of others, and the desire to do this is the test of whether we are in charge of our lives or if the quest for power dominates us.

A god named wealth.   A God who created us in love provided us with a beautiful world. Out of that same love flows
an abundance of material things to be enjoyed and shared.
Respectful use of these things can relax and renew us, can
bring us happiness and heal our bodies and souls. To have
more of the goods of this earth does not necessarily mean that
we are unfaithful to a God at whose hands we received them.

The question is the place that these things hold in our
lives. The question is one related to the power that may come
to us with accumulated wealth.

The ultimate question revolves around our willingness to
pay the price that is demanded to give direction to life and to
discover its center which is God.

A god named security.   If "safety first" is our primary pre-
cept we will never be earnestly involved in the risky pursuit of
the meaning of life. To find the truth often involves letting go
of some untruth. To question requires both energy and an
openness to what we discover.

Our best role model is Jesus. He was clearly a high-risk
person. His choices about the way he lived and with whom
and in what way he would share life placed him often at the
margins of society. Staying alive with a commitment to become more and more alive is risky business. Jesus lost his life
so that we might better find ours. Following such an example
does not allow us the luxury of continual security but it does
hold a promise of greater life.

A god named -ism.   We find in words like materialism,
racism or sexism, a base that is, of itself, good. Adding the
-ism, according to the dictionary, involves a doctrine, theory
or system with implications that are often disparaging.

The goodness of the -ism is related to the position it oc-
cupies in the life of the person involved. Has it replaced the
center of life so that all else stands in relationship to it, so that
no other truth has meaning or value apart from it? When and
if this happens, it has truly become a god for us.

A feminist who forgets the shared quest for full life for

both men and women has set feminism in a place that properly belongs only to the two great commandments.

A god named pain removal. No one likes to hurt. But, pain is a reality for human life. There is more of it present in some lives than in others. Any form of preoccupation with the conviction that life ought to be free of pain is calculated to result in frustration and in the loss of valuable energy for seeking the meaning that is hidden in the pain that is a part of every person's life.

We carry expectations that others can and must either prevent or immediately remove our pain. Certainly our present age of litigation is indicative of a need to make someone else responsible for and the cause of suffering that is often unavoidable.

This kind of anger with pain speaks to some expectation we carry that we ought never hurt, that if we live right and/or have enough money to buy it, some kind of help can either prevent pain or remove it immediately.

A god named acclaim. This god arises out of some distortion of a real good or a healthy need. The desire to be loved sometimes leads to a demand. The desire to be accepted for who we are sometimes becomes a preoccupation with being acclaimed for being more than we are.

Acclaim, popularity, and recognition sometimes become so important to us that we lack the energy required to discover our gifts so that we can become the best of who we are. The undue need for acclaim, popularity and recognition can place a pressure on us that may result in our either compromising or giving away who we are so that we might possess them. When we do this, we have lost our lives, but not in the way of which Jesus spoke when he said, "To find your life you sometimes have to lose it."

Freedom From These False Gods

How shall we finally become free of the enslavement of

these false gods? How shall we become faithful followers of a
God of unconditional love and unfailing forgiveness?

In the book of Isaiah we read:

> The Spirit of Lord Yahweh is on me
> for Yahweh has anointed me.
> He has sent me to bring the news to the afflicted,
> to soothe the broken-hearted,
> to proclaim liberty to captives,
> release to those in prison (Is 61:1).

Who will set us free of our inclinations to gravitate toward false gods because we fear the effort involved in discovering and then following God? Who shall help us let go of the
"precepts picked from the garbage cans of older people" that
Lillian Hellman speaks of so clearly and fearsomely? How
shall we come to believe that, while the quest for the God of
life can never be easy, it has its inner rewards not able to be
tasted by those who resist the journey?

Several factors are involved in our becoming free within
and without. Among these are:

1. Our need for information
2. Our need to trust our own experience through self-
   reflection
3. Some good companions along the way including
   trustworthy guides and cherished friends.

Many people who call themselves "practicing, believing Catholics" today know very little about their church or its teach-
ings. They have done little studying of either scripture or theology, have little knowledge of the history that has brought the
church to its present position with regard to the truth revealed
in the bible, its practice of the sacraments or its understanding of itself. Many adults have little more than the catechism
knowledge they memorized as children.

Many want to blame the changes that have followed in

the wake of the Second Vatican Council as the cause of their confusion and disillusion. If the changes caused confusion, it is most likely not the changes themselves but the fact that there was not a good solid base of understanding before the changes which is at the heart of their anger. The call to be an informed Christian carries with it an urgency and an opportunity for people to begin to free themselves of their own obstacles to life through, with, and in God.

Most of us grew up believing that there are two ways in which God's presence among us is revealed — through scripture and through tradition. But God's presence is also revealed through the human experience and through reflection on the meaning of that experience. Each of us is, in the end, our own best authority on the truth of the life that God has given to us. Widening the spheres for revelation works together with a personal process of self-discovery and a well-developed set of inner instincts to strengthen belief in self. Trusting that God's love and life are revealed through our own efforts to love and to live helps free us from the gods within and without that would rob us of the possibility of an inner-determined and self-directed life.

We will not go through the painful process of freeing ourselves from the enslavement of any form of false god if we attempt to do this in isolation. We travel best in the companionship of others.

Along the way we need trustworthy guides who announce to us the good news about the God who is, guides who reach to bind our wounds and heal our hearts of life's inevitable hurts. Along the way we need the presence of friends who offer us unconditional love and unfailing forgiveness. St. John reminded us that no one has ever seen God and that the test of God's presence among us is in our love and care for one another.

When we seek to invest well in the threefold relationship that is a given for our lives, we will no longer be captives of false gods but will walk free to respond to the God who is.

6 The Tragedy of Folded-Up Lives

I want to unfold
I don't want to stay folded anywhere,
because where I am folded
There I am a lie.

Selected Poems, Rainer Maria Rilke

The needless suffering and personal destruction that flow from a preoccupation with envy is revealed in the movie based on Peter Shaffer's play *Amadeus*. While we might expect that the author would simply have told the story of Mozart, one of the world's gifted composers, we discover that the central themes focus on the power of a court composer named Salieri to harm Mozart and to influence the responses of their contemporaries.

Mozart's creativity and his naivete made him vulnerable to the envy of the wily Salieri, while his pride and boorish denigration of Salieri's talent made him a more likely victim.

Eventually Salieri proclaims his desire to break Mozart. While crediting his musical genius, Salieri invests his energy in harming Mozart in whatever ways he can. In return, Salieri receives a short-lived fame and the fortune he seeks, but leaves a heritage of uninspired work. And Mozart receives musical immortality.

Salieri's overriding desire to destroy Mozart eventually leads to his musical demise. Because he remains preoccupied with envy, his own talents are undeveloped. The contribution Salieri might have made to the world of music was never realized.

Mozart suffers greatly at Salieri's hands but his musical excellence cannot be touched. Out of his suffering and in relation to it, Mozart produced even greater music. The wondrous gifts that he received from the creator — *Amadeus* means "love of God" — linked with his untiring efforts to share his music, made him into what Shaffer calls "God's musical flute."

The creative genius of one flowered while that of the other remained, as Rilke's words suggest, "folded up." Mozart's desire to give expression to his celebration of life remained undaunted despite the obstacles Salieri set in his path, whatever kind of personal suffering resulted.

Had Salieri sufficiently respected and cherished his own talents, had he used his energy to give expression to his own gifts, the world might have enjoyed another musical heritage. In the end, Salieri's sin of refusal destroyed him. His sin was not so much in harm done, but in good left undone. His life did not unfold.

Redefining Sin

Our common understanding of sin is related to breaking laws, to offenses committed, to wrongs done against self and others. We tend to think of the harm done by sinning to be the result of decisions to do something we should not do.

The old catechism, which some of us grew up with as a primer for Christian life and belief, defines sin as "Any willful thought, desire, word, action, or omission forbidden by the law of God." But, as that definition has been practiced, it is once again clear that the focus for sin has been mainly on actions performed, and, to some lesser extent, on harmful words spoken.

The old moral theology books usually emphasized "sins of the body" and these dealt with sexuality. Such a limited focus has hindered our approach to relationships and has postponed our understanding of the goodness and beauty of human sexuality. It has made nearly inaccessible information that would free us to explore the deepest meaning of our sexuality and the power and creativity that are centered in it.

I remember hearing a lecture given by Richard McCormick, a gifted American theologian, in which he said, "To the extent that we begin by moralizing about something, we cannot discover its true morality." I believe that nowhere is this more true than in our approach to the possibility of finally unveiling the goodness and strength that are related to an acceptance of the human condition and the centrality of sexuality in personhood. Unless and until we take more note of and grow more aware of the word "omission" in our understanding of sin, we cannot claim to be faithful to the two great commandments.

The poets have asked questions and written about omission — door not opened, roads not walked, dreams not pursued. They lead us to ask questions about good not done, words never spoken, gifts never developed.

The media reminds us daily of the thousands of evil deeds done, of lives destroyed by the actions of others. Who challenges us with the deeds not done by which the lives of others are equally destroyed? Who calls us to free ourselves from the temptation to allow our lives to remain folded up because of our insecurity or cowardice in risking for a more complete and more fully human life?

Some Virtues to Be Cultivated If Life Is to Unfold

Part of the pain involved in being fully alive is that life does not unfold by itself. If we are to grow, to change, to respond to our life experiences then there are inevitable risks to be taken and vulnerabilities to be accepted.

If we refuse to respond to the life around us, if we choose to isolate ourselves from it by seeking certainty and security, we will be like the people described in God's word as "people who walk in darkness." Jesus offers the promise, "I am the light of the world; anyone who follows me will not be walking in the dark" (Jn 8:12). St. Paul reminds us:

> You were darkness once, but now you are light in the
> Lord; behave as children of light, for the effects of the
> light are seen in complete goodness and uprightness
> and truth (Eph 5:8-9).

Just as we have grown up with certain definitions of sin,
so we have had another set of virtues held up to us. Among
these are perfection, consistency, self-assurance, freedom from
failure, strength, and clarity. The extent to which these have
harmed us is related to our ability to accept their opposites
when, after having done all that we knew how to do, we were
not always able to attain some goal or perform in ways we had
expected of ourselves.

Just as I have been shaped by those who love me and
those who do not, so also I am what I am due to my acceptance of my gifts and limitations. Failure adds a richness to life
that success cannot.

Reflecting on this leads me to a list of "virtues" or qualities I find that draw me to people and give me an added measure of confidence in them. I know that I would never choose
to take counsel with a person, however acclaimed, who con-
veys the evident message of never having failed, never having
suffered from confusion or fear.

Qualities are related to the circumstances or events that
have touched the insides as well as the outsides of our lives.
They are tension-related virtues for they are born of the suffering that is inseparable from discovering and conditioning
life. They are virtues that make it a bit more possible for us to
celebrate the goodness of life as we discover some of the common bonds that make life-sharing more meaningful.

Self-doubt. I have met people who communicated an air
of absolute confidence in themselves. Questioning themselves
seemed never to occur to them. Whatever other feelings I may

have had about them, one thing struck me strongly. I wondered what place friends had in such a clearly ordered life.

For me, one important role of a friend is to sometimes serve as a second set of eyes, seeing what I have failed to notice; a second set of ears, picking up sounds whose subtlety has evaded me. A healthy amount of self-doubt and self-questioning leaves room for a friend.

Powerlessness.   Power is a gift. It makes it possible to help make good things happen for ourselves, for others and for our world. God's creative power fashioned this lovely world in which we live.

For human beings to be always in a position of power is to risk having the gift destroyed, for power can also corrupt. To continually be in a position of power sometimes makes it nearly impossible for good people to identify with the powerlessness of others in such a way as to manifest a genuine concern or a willingness to help liberate others.

A painful experience of powerlessness — of not being in control of a situation — such as divorce, job loss, or the terminal illness of a loved one, offers the possibility of greater sensitivity to and identification with others.

Acceptance of failure.   I believe there is no person who does not prefer success to failure. Those of us who plan and prepare for decisions and events expect that our efforts will be rewarded. When something unforeseen or unknown forces the turn of events in an unpredicted direction, we are surprised, disappointed and angry.

Learning to accept the fact that careful planning is no insurance against failure and that failure does not make us failures as persons is an important lesson.

I was not surprised to read in a description of suicide among young people that people who have never failed at anything important to them may be likely prospects for suicide. Among those who actually do take their own lives, a significant number do so in the wake of some first disappointing personal failure related to school, job or relationship.

Having failed at something gives us an increased empathy for people whose lives are more like a never-ending series of failures. A part of discovering some meaning in the pain of failure is to accept it as a part of every person's humanness.

Dealing with rejection.   No one is universally accepted and loved. The more we strive to walk in the light, to unfold and grow, the more probability there is that we will be rejected by some and not understood by others.

Rejection is painful, but buying acceptability at the price of who we are is even more painful. When we are able to share an experience of having been rejected, we are rewarded by realizing that the pain involved has given us bonds borne of suffering.

Vulnerability.   Vulnerability is a quality that endears because it is a manifestation of trust. Occasionally I meet a person who seems to be invulnerable, stonelike. There is a coldness, an inflexibility that speaks of an inability or a refusal to be open to others and to life. Such people are not attractive as warm companions with whom I might wish to share a piece of the journey.

Some measure of inconsistency.   Striving for consistent response to our process of self-discovery and to our faithfulness in relationships is a quality that invites us to feel good about ourselves. To be consistent in our feelings and in our dealings with others makes our lives more predictable and more comfortable. But to give consistency so high a priority that we refuse to allow any inconsistencies may result in a lack of tolerance of others. It may even put us in the position of feeling free to judge others harshly.

An awareness of our inconsistencies can make us more tolerant of and patient with the sometimes irksome inconsistencies in the lives of others. If one of our goals is to love and accept others, then accepting and recognizing the discrepancies that are a part of us serves as a good basis.

A sense of our sinfulness. While sin is not a popular word even in some churches, and a too much used word in others, it does exist. Women and men can and do sin. We can and do fail ourselves and others. We are capable not only of sins of frailty, but even of malice. We sometimes sin in the darkness of not knowing or fully understanding, but we do sometimes sin with knowledge and clear intention.

A little inventory-taking will make us aware of our ability to rationalize, our ways of seeking to make others less than they are, our hidden delight when someone who has hurt us is now hurting.

While not wanting to live mainly out of an "I am not worthy" stance towards life which denies our gifts, we are called to acknowledge our need for forgiveness. Needing forgiveness always from someone for something is one of the things we share in common as creatures of a loving God who stands always ready to forgive us.

Our refusal to accept who we are as human beings, with all that this involves, will eventually break us just as it did Salieri. We will be broken by refusals to speak life-giving words, to touch with healing hands, to be gentle with ourselves. We must make the sometimes arduous journey in self-discovery or there can be no self-cherishing and no offering the gift of self in relationships.

By contrast, I think of a woman named Connie who I came to know while she was in treatment for chemical dependency. She had gone there against her will but with no denial of her problem. Her stay at the treatment center was the longest on record.

She called and asked me to visit her which I did regularly through those weeks. What her brilliant mind and her nearly broken heart knew, her fear of the future sought to reject. Exchanging patterns of self-destruction and self-deprecation for self-knowledge and self-love would not be easy for Connie.

She told me that all the testimonials given by sober and

recovering alcoholics were not yet enough. For her to change had ramifications for her marriage. The prospect of finding new social circles seemed so overwhelming as to appear hopelessly impossible.

One day, with Connie's permission, I invited a woman to go to the treatment center with me who was facing the truth that her long-term separation was going to end in divorce. Both women were hurting, each was in need of some new friends. As their visits became more frequent each realized that, though the outer circumstances of their suffering seemed very different, what was happening inside of them was not that different.

Each could have refused the gift the other had to offer. Necessity seemed not to allow them to close the door on a possible new place of support and care at a time when each needed exactly that. They were not long in discovering the power of the common bonds they shared, bonds born of need but not ending there.

Each could have refused the life offered. Each recognized that by the standards of their lives before these events, they would have been perceived as having little in common. Both knew that neither would have been as ready for her future without the presence of the other.

Taking Another Look at Some Old Definitions

To each event and circumstance of life we bring a personal history. That history includes our parents, brothers and sisters, the teachers we had and the education that is now ours. It includes the cities in which we grew up and the places we have visited. We make decisions against the backdrop which is the tapestry of our life.

We have grown up seeing and listening to the ways in which others respond to life and we have established our personal responses to situations. We hold a set of beliefs that shape both our value system and our behavior.

We have listened to others who taught us about God and lived a certain way because they believed in the truth revealed in the life of Jesus. We learned that certain ways of acting were pleasing to God and others were not. We may have been taught to rely more on our catechism than on our bible. We may have learned to memorize answers more efficiently than we learned to discover life's important questions.

Most of us who grew up Catholic, perhaps other Christians, too, memorized what we called the seven capital sins. We learned that they were the chief sources of sin, the chief reasons why women and men commit sin.

I am not suggesting that we ought not have learned these things, but I am saying that if we lack the motivation to continually rethink our faith we discover that we are carrying numerous precepts that are not life-giving. To try to live a mature commitment out of a child's knowledge presents serious difficulties for those who wish to grow in their faith. It is to have a folded-up faith life.

Respect for our personal past and for whatever journey we have made in our faith invites us to respect the fact that the church has and is making its own journey with us. We, like the church, must grow in our understanding of what life in Christ means. Our faith life, like our professional life, sometimes needs in-service training and continuing education.

Sometimes we just need to take a new look at some familiar words to see if we can gain new insights. Sometimes it is both helpful and liberating to remind ourselves that we get lost along the way because we fail to provide new sources of light. And so it is with the word sin.

It might be helpful, if we have mainly thought of sin as something we do or commit, to widen it with some reflection on sin as what we fail to do, sin as refusal to live, as refusal to allow our lives to unfold. The self-destructiveness of "sin as refusal" may be apparent to us if we consider the long-term effects of the following:

- refusing to choose out of fear or insecurity
- refusing to listen to and trust the messages of personal life experience
- refusing to let go of a "safety first," "right answer for life" stance
- refusing to deal with our unrealistic expectations of ourselves and others
- refusing to accept our humanness
- refusing to admit that we can and do sin
- refusing to tell the truth to ourselves and others
- refusing to rid ourselves of the power of half-truths
- refusing to take responsibility for our own lives and abdicating to another.

Our refusals deprive us of life; they allow us to remain uninvolved in the process of growing. Whatever mistakes we make are easily healed in contrast to the ultimate destruction of being spectators to our own lives and to the world. The poet Yevtushenko says in *Stolen Apples* that "It's a disgrace to be free of your age. A hundred times more shameful than to be its slave."

Look at the seven sources of sin, as defined in the Baltimore Catechism No. 2. Then look at that same sin from the perspective of something we do or do not do or some inner attitude we lack.

PRIDE—*Too great an opinion of ourselves*

Might we not think of this as a . . .
- self-righteousness born of an inadequate self-image?
- refusal to acknowledge our own brokenness while magnifying and even rejoicing in that of others?
- refusal to cherish our humanness that flows over

into a desire to play at being god or angel?

— refusal to accept the fact that we have limitations which make it difficult to accept that others also have their limitations?

— belief that we either can or ought to be able to remove the pain present in the lives of others?

— failure to believe that we are lovable, capable, gifted?

COVETOUSNESS—*Too great love or desire for earthly goods.*

Isn't the implication that covetousness relates primarily to things outside of ourselves too limited and limiting a definition? Isn't it also . . .

— preoccupation with pain removal, feeling better instantly?

— seeking instant gratification, immediate reward?

— clutching and clinging to another in a relationship rather than approaching with openness and with more realistic expectations?

— choosing security as a way of life, fearing to place ourselves in a position where we must let go of something or someone?

— wanting to possess things or persons too easily and too quickly and, perhaps, without investing anything of ourselves?

— demanding quick, easy answers to life's unanswered and sometimes unanswerable questions?

— accumulating friends as if they were things, and things as though we had no need of friends?

LUST—*The desire for bodily pleasure that is sinful or impure.*

Does not this definition make the surface of a
relationship seem more important than the inside?
Isn't lust also . . .

— using another in relationship?

— physical exploitation, even if mutual?

— giving self away in relationship so as to have or
  keep the friend?

— lacking respect for, inability to cherish one another
  for the gift each is?

— lacking sensitivity to the feelings of another?

— lacking reverence for ourselves?

— failing to believe that friendship is, primarily, a
  sharing of all of life and not just of bodies?

*ANGER—Loss of temper for no good reason,
hatred and revenge, wanting to get even.*

Do we not need to separate feelings of anger from
acting out of angry feelings in destructive ways?
Doesn't anger also mean . . .

— refusing to accept the fact that life is not fair?

— undue exasperation because of the failings of
  others?

— refusing to deal with the feelings which may result
  in our either clinging to them or acting them out
  in some inappropriate way?

— refusing to accept change?

— frustration with our faults and idiosyncracies and
  those of others?

— refusing to accept the fact that we cannot always be
  in control of people and/or things?

— doing continual battle with life, growth, and
  change?

*GLUTTONY—Drinking or eating too much, or
with too great haste or desire.*

Why have we restricted this to the use of food and
drink? Why not think of it as an inner attitude that
has much wider applications? Isn't it also . . .

— failure to be grateful for and to revere all the good
gifts that God has given us?

— failure to enjoy and to celebrate the good use of
food and its place in friendship as food is shared?

— selfishly desiring to accumulate friends in quantity
rather than noticing the quality of our relationships?

— refusing to invest deeply in any relationship while
allowing ourselves to be superficial in many?

— deluging others with gifts and words, rather than
letting them free in their responses?

— using words carelessly or excessively?

— being overly conscious of making good impressions
for their own sake rather than for the sake of a
relationship?

*ENVY—Jealousy, being sad at another's good or
success.*

Cannot envy be manifested in our refusals to speak
and to offer affirmation because of our poor self-
image? Cannot envy be a . . .

— refusal to affirm the gifts of another as though this
takes something away from us?

— refusal to speak the words to another that recognize their gifts?

— refusal to tell others of the gifts of a friend, of their
abilities?

— means to find ways to make others appear less than
  they are?

— means to find ways to make ourselves seem more
  than we are?

— unreal or unrealistic sense of our own gifts?

— lack of reverence for our own gifts?

SLOTH—A laziness that makes us neglect our duty.

Why have we failed to believe that we can be lazy
about the inward journey as well as the outward
ones? Aren't we slothful when we . . .

— refuse to make the costly choices that will best free
  and develop the gifts that are ours?

— become a workaholic so that we will free ourselves
  of the responsibility to do the hard work that is
  involved in self-discovery and self-sharing?

— stay busy socializing so that we will not have to
  commit ourselves to the cost of intimacy?

— refuse to pray, to look inward so that we can more
  effectively share our lives with others?

— care more for the easy outer goals than for the
  quest for inner integrity?

— do not invest energy in rethinking our faith, our
  values, our goals?

— do not care enough for ourselves to seek the life to
  the full to which Jesus calls us?

We need to develop convictions that remind us that sinning,
that refusing to unfold and respond to God's call to life is as
much a matter of inner attitudes as of the actions we do. Jesus' clear statement that the kingdom is within is a reminder

that life is an inside-out process. As Michael Crosby writes in *Spirituality of the Beatitudes:*

> External sins did not matter that much to Jesus, although he brought healing to them. What concerned Jesus about them was that they revealed a brokenness at the base of life. There God could not be found.

When we choose to live less of life than we might, to set restrictions on life's possibilities for ourselves or others, we will surely suffer. We may also destroy.

When we take risks that we believe are for life, we will certainly suffer but will also reap rich inner rewards. Risk induces anxiety. It is filled with abundant tension, but this is how we grow more conscious of who we are, who God is, and of how important those who love us are to us.

Making a Commitment to Life to the Full

One of the difficulties in following in the footsteps of Jesus is that while we are attracted to the clarity and simplicity of his stories and principles, we may be temporarily distracted from the price we will have to pay if we seek his long-term companionship. We may too easily accept the vision of life that Jesus offers and then, later, refuse to live by it because it will necessarily involve us in suffering as it did for him.

William Faulkner wrote, "If I had to choose between pain and no feeling, I would choose pain." We might add that choosing between pain and no feeling is a part of the decision we make when we choose life, some life, less life or the full life which God promised us.

The occasional accounts of people who search for sunken treasures off the coastal regions of the United States reveal men and women with a sense of adventure and a willingness to risk failure. Their clear commitment is admirable and inspiring. They possess the kind of courage described by Martin Luther King, Jr.:

Courage is an inner resolution to go forward despite
obstacles; Cowardice is submissive surrender to circumstances. Courage breeds creative self-affirmation;
Cowardice produces destructive self-abnegation.
Courage faces fear and masters it; Cowardice re-
presses fear and is mastered by it.

The search for the hidden treasures buried on ships on
the ocean floor, and the inner attitudes of those who carry it
out, bear strong similarity to each person's quest to discover
the hidden self. The same sense of adventure and quality of
personal investment is required.

If we lack a sense of inner adventure, lack a willingness
to risk for life, lack a resolve that wins out over pain and obstacles along the way, we will not likely find our own hidden
treasures. If we refuse to stretch and go beyond where we are
now or beyond what we possess now, if we give ourselves excuses for not doing this, we will have paid a high price for a
lesser life. Courage is one of the keys that unlocks those areas
that must be opened if our lives are ever to unfold.

7 The Virtue of the Brave

> Forgiveness is the virtue of the brave. He alone is
> strong enough to avenge a wrong who knows how to
> love (and forgive).
>
> Gandhi

Gene and Terry grew up in the same neighborhood. They
were best friends through high school. They were college
roommates. Now, after graduation, they were being separated
for the first time because Terry had taken a position with a
large corporation in a distant city.

They decided to take one last trip together and they
chose some of the New Hampshire hiking trails as the place to
share their memories and their dreams.

For some reason not fully understood by either, the time
on the mountain trails did not go well. They agreed to end
their vacation early and return home. They parted with few
words and no effort at reconciliation.

Terry told me later that as the weeks and months passed,
he often thought of calling Gene and asking to meet him
somewhere halfway between the two cities in which they
worked. So painful did he find the disappointment of their uncomfortable time together, a time which he had hoped would
cement forever their bonds, that when he picked up the
phone, he placed it back on its cradle without ever dialing
Gene's number.

About two years later I saw Terry again at his parents'
home. He was sad, withdrawn, and seemed somewhat de-

pressed. I had never before seen him in what appeared to be such a hopeless state.

When we were finally alone I asked him how his new job was going and when he planned to be married (having just heard of his engagement). I was not prepared for his response. With a tone of sadness and regret he said quietly, "Gene was killed instantly in an automobile accident a month ago."

In his tear-filled eyes I could read not only the pain of loss, but the agony of helplessness and lost opportunity. When he could finally speak, one question after another tumbled out. Why was I so stubborn? Why didn't I go to him? Why didn't we care enough to try to do something before we parted in New Hampshire? How can this ever be healed now? He was my best friend. How can I ever forgive myself?

Now, several years later, Terry still carries with him reminders of a reconciliation that did not happen. He has let go of some of the whys, but not all of them.

In retrospect, Terry believes that an ailing relationship might have been healed had he offered four simple words to Gene. Asking the question, "Will you forgive me?" would have placed no blame, would have implied no malice. It would have implied neither right nor wrong. It would have opened the door to welcome the love of a friend.

I sensed no undue assumption of blame when Terry said, "If I had been more faithful to myself and to our friendship, I would have allowed my remorse to lead me to seek forgiveness. Nothing would have mattered but doing whatever I could to let Gene know how important he was to me." Then he added, "Even if he couldn't forgive, I would have felt better about myself and wouldn't be living with so much self-doubt."

Part of the curious nature of forgiveness is that it affects both the one who seeks it and the one who gives it. The words we pray in the "Our Father" exact a difficult commitment by their reminder that we are asking to be forgiven as we forgive. The willingness to offer and to receive forgiveness may reveal more of strength and inner courage than do most other facets of friendship and of life. Dietrich von Hildebrand in his classic volume, *Fundamental Moral Attitudes*, writes:

> . . . What is realized and what shines forth in an act of real forgiveness, in a noble and generous renunciation, in a burning and selfless love, is more significant and noble, more important and eternal than all cultural values.

The story of Gene and Terry is not a sad one for me. I believe that somehow, through the mystery of God's love and the love two good men had for one another, their reconciliation has happened. I also believe that the story is a hope-filled reminder to each of us that Gandhi is right when he calls forgiveness "the virtue of the brave."

Terry's recounting of the story invited me to ask some questions about both the nature of forgiveness and some of the forgiveness experiences of my life. I have talked with others about what forgiveness means to them and the importance they give to the process of learning to forgive and seeking forgiveness.

Each conversation reminded me that forgiveness involves risk and renewed security in a relationship. It includes discovering more about both myself and another. The process of forgiveness is never easy and can never be taken for granted.

Some Questions About Forgiveness

Literature and history tell us the stories of men and women whose decisions were greatly affected by unhealed wounds and unforgiven deeds. Families and nations have suffered because people were unwilling or unable to be reconciled. What is not reconciled sets up currents that flow outward and become more powerful the longer they remain unleashed.

Forgiveness, on the other hand, is a gentling experience for the one who offers it and for the one who receives it. It prepares people to enter into the suffering and uncertainty of the lives of others.

Who is healed most, the one who forgives or the one forgiven? Neither. Both are healed, but in different ways. Seeking forgiveness, standing in need of forgiveness, changes our stance before another. Offering forgiveness in a way that does not strip another of his or her worth opens the doors to possible new life for the relationship and for both persons. To be forgiven and to be forgiving adds some beautifying quality to life that makes us at once vulnerable and strong, cautious and brave.

The act of forgiveness highlights the common denominators that bond us and allows us to be more accepting of the differences that sometimes divide us.

The act of forgiveness may not be a one-step process. Sometimes the best we can do is gradually let go of disappointment and bitterness, while feeling a bit more whole with each step.

Can We Help Our Unwillingness to Forgive?

I recently watched a story on television about two men whose bitter refusal to be reconciled threatened to destroy them both, their families and their businesses. Their stubborn pride prevented them from seeing beyond personal setbacks and led each to make unfounded judgments. Sadly, the truth that might have made them friends never came to light until one had died. The two men were trapped in a lifelong pursuit of power and acclaim that brought them the poverty of unbending wills and unforgiving hearts.

The only obstacles to reconciliation that any of us can deal with and seek to remove are our own. A good beginning is taking a personal inventory and prayer. An important motivator to forgiving is to recognize the power we give someone whom we are unwilling to forgive.

Jesus' statement, "Forgive and you will be forgiven," was a clear call to be a forgiving person. It was also a reminder of our responsibility to insure our own forgiveness.

> Yes, if you forgive others their failings, your heavenly Father will forgive you yours; but if you do not forgive others, your Father will not forgive your failings either (Mt 6:14-15).

The act of forgiving is singularly unique and essential. It flows out of inner attitudes that touch all of life and not just those in need of being reconciled. Refusing to forgive or seek forgiveness may destroy more of life than any other single choice we make.

When Forgiveness Happens, What Makes It Possible?

Some reflection will remind us of several important facets of forgiveness. Each plays some part in preparing us to be forgiving people.

Forgiveness is one of our most humanizing needs. Forgiving people have a quality that helps us feel at home with them. In their presence we are comfortable. With them we feel safe. They stand in contrast to the righteous and unforgiving who convey the message that we need or ought to be punished for being who we are or for what we have done. We wish to emulate the forgiving presence and to avoid being like the judging person.

Forgiving people strengthen us with the unconditional love and acceptance they offer. We instinctively seek to share their gift to us with others.

When we seek forgiveness from someone we love, we notice that more is removed than one single barrier. It is as though the removal of one obstacle carries away others we may not have been aware of. The flood of healing that sweeps through us carries away some of our darkness and fears.

Whatever price is involved in seeking forgiveness, whatever pain is involved is quickly forgotten when we hear the lovingly liberating words "I forgive you."

What Happens to Us When Forgiveness Is Refused?

Perhaps only someone who has relied on a love that proved conditional, or sought forgiveness that was denied, can describe the depths of such disappointment.

In trusting the truth of what we believed to be a good relationship, we find the pain greatly multiplied when we are rejected instead of supported, or when the doors to reconciliation are closed for reasons we do not understand.

The barriers that separate us from someone we love are difficult to live with as we continue to hear the words, "Let it be for now. It needs time and distance."

We are painfully stretched beyond anything we have experienced when the openness we were certain of has become a barrier we are powerless to touch, much less remove. Faithful watching and waiting for the right time is not much comfort. Perhaps we are afraid that there will not be a time. We have heard too many stories like that of Gene and Terry.

How Does Forgiveness Feel?

There may be no more freeing truth than that of a love that forgives and removes another's burden. Those who have been forgiven share the common feeling that a weight has been lifted.

One woman told me, at a retreat weekend, that she felt like she had been scrubbed clean inside when she could finally forgive her husband several years after their divorce. She said that she felt like the accumulations of years of anger and blaming were finally gone, and that she could now share his concern for their children without competitive games.

A man whose wife had been killed by a Japanese soldier during World War II said that it has taken him more than 40 years to be able to look at an Oriental face without bitterness and with no desire for revenge. He described what a terrible loss of energy it was for him to have felt hatred toward a whole race of people. He said that he carried this heavy burden until fairly recently when a Japanese specialist saved the life of his brother in a West Coast medical center.

Refusing or not knowing how to offer forgiveness are obstacles to intimacy. Small but unhealed hurts that have grown into gnawing resentments are common barriers to the growth of a friendship. The accumulation of seemingly insignificant but unreconciled hurts may sap the life and deface the beauty of relationships that are meant to be life-sustaining.

The removal of these obstacles, the giving and receiving of forgiveness, releases powerful energy that results in unpredicted new growth together and reveals the hitherto unrealized power of the love.

It takes courage to offer and receive forgiveness because, if the barrier that now separates us is removed, we are again and perhaps even more vulnerable to one another. We can hurt one another again.

But we can also love one another more. We can share life more fully because we have been faithful to ourselves and to another. Because we have been faithful to God's clear promise that we will be forgiven as we forgive, we are better receptors of the full promise of life — the reward of those who seek to love through forgiving.

From Whom Do We Need Forgiveness?

The two great commandments are a clear statement of the threefold nature of relationships as they enjoin us to love God above all else and to love our neighbor as ourselves. These same commandments remind us that forgiveness is a matter of three sets of relationships that are a part of every life.

Few of us would question our need for forgiveness from

God, but many of us interfere with that process by either failing to believe that God forgives or by failing to accept the unconditional acceptance that is ours by reason of being God's
creatures.

How often do we hear someone say, "There is no point
in my praying ever again. I know that God will never forgive
me for what I have done." It is we who, by inner attitudes reflected in such a statement, refuse to acknowledge a God
present to us always. We give up on God. God does not give
up on us. He does not set us apart when we have sinned, loving us less. We set the barriers; we fail to believe in God's loving ways.

Our refusal to love a forgiving God may increase our difficulty in believing that any kind of forgiveness is possible.
But, our relationship with God can be affected by never having experienced the unconditional love and unfailing faithfulness of another person.

Relationships are interconnected. We love our neighbor
more generously and with greater tenderness if we believe in
God and seek to be faithful to the life we are called to. We are
more likely to believe in God's love when that love has been
revealed to us through family and friends in whose life we
share and whose forgiveness we have received.

We do need forgiveness from God and from one another.
How freely that loving forgiveness can flow to and through us,
is intimately related to and dependent upon our relationship
with ourselves. People who have a poor self-image find it very
difficult to seek forgiveness; they also refuse to believe that
their forgiveness will really make a difference to anyone else.

A woman named Sharon once told me that shortly after
her divorce was final, she had begun to go to bed with a man
she scarcely knew much less loved. She described those
months as a total waste and the relationship as a mutual exploitation. She said she finally ended the involvement only because she was afraid that her teenage children would find out
about it.

She cried while telling her story and said that she had never told anyone what had happened. Nor had she gone near a church. She was sure God would not forgive her.

She continued to cry and there was silence for a while before she said, "So what are you thinking?" I was thinking what a heavy burden this was because it was unshared. When I spoke I asked her, "Sharon, is God the problem?"

As the tears continued to stream down her face she waited a long time before she could speak. Then she broke into nearly uncontrollable sobbing and I could scarcely understand her words, "No, not really. I have never been able to forgive myself. I have never liked myself. I have never been very successful at anything that I have done and, when my marriage ended, it seemed to me to be a proof that I was not worth loving."

I believe that at the heart of all loving and, therefore, of forgiving, is the effort to invest whatever energy is required to come to know and love ourselves. I believe that all loving and forgiving flows out of us, out of the center in us where we know and love and forgive ourselves. It is a costly process of which we speak, one which will bring us to greater openness to God's rule of forgiveness as Christopher Fry describes it in *A Sleep of Prisoners:*

> . . . We are afraid to live by the rule of God which is forgiveness, mercy, and compassion, fearing that by these we shall be ended. And yet if we could bear these three through dread and terror and terror's doubt, daring to return good for evil, without thought of what will come, I cannot think we should be losers.

All too often we are the last and least recipients of our compassion, mercy and forgiveness. Dread and terror arise from our doubts about who we are and whether or not we are lovable.

Who Is the Forgiving Person?

There are few people who are not concerned about whether or not they are attractive to others. There are few people who do not instinctively gravitate toward certain personality types. We say that "likes attract," but we also know that we are attracted to people who have qualities that we wish we had. We do this in the hope that we might learn to develop those qualities in ourselves.

Good people are drawn to the goodness manifested in the lives of other good people. We notice what it is about them that makes us want to be in their presence.

I believe that genuinely forgiving people have certain qualities that are born of suffering and for which they have paid a high price. We are not compassionate, forgiving people simply by reason of our birth. We learn to forgive as we learn to love, beginning with early role models, continuing through life experiences and with reflection on the ways in which we respond.

Compassion is not a gift. It is an attractive quality that we may wish to choose for our lives. Like courage, it is born of a series of choices we make to forgive or not forgive, to love or not to love. Courage, along with love and forgiveness, shows itself in adversity.

Forgiving people are attractive to other good people because they are aware of their need for forgiveness, of their difficulty in seeking it, and of their suffering when it has been refused or delayed.

There is a personal discipline involved in becoming a person who forgives. Learning to do the difficult, choosing to risk being hurt, seeking the vulnerable place we put ourselves in when we forgive is learned only with repetition. It necessarily precludes ever setting ourselves in the position of judging another.

People who are not good listeners are not likely to be ready to forgive. Listening to the truth of life goes beyond hearing words. Listening for the context in which a life is lived makes allowances not made by those who see things as black and white, clear and certain. Those able to hear the nuances of life have developed a gift that has been fine-tuned through their own experiences of living and through their commitment to reflect on those experiences.

Forgiving people are willing to accept others as they are. They place no unrealistic expectations on others, give no messages that begin with "should" or "ought." Rather they manifest a willingness to walk with us so that we might grow to some better place of life.

When I think of the qualities of a forgiving person, I am reminded of a conversation at a weekend workshop. Each of us was asked who we would seek out if we were dealing with something in our lives that needed healing and forgiveness. One person said that she would not seek a holy counsellor but rather an intelligent and perceptive one. Another said that he would not look at the person's education but rather at his life experience. A young man said that he would seek an older person because older people usually were wiser. I said that I would seek a person who had been through some period of profound suffering because I believe that compassion is born of pain.

The lives of people like Gandhi give witness to this central place of suffering. He said that he believed that prayer was not about asking for either food or forgiveness. He believed that prayer begins in the longing of the soul and with a daily admission of our own limitations and weaknesses. It is better, he said, to have a heart without words than to share words that have no heart. For Gandhi, as for us, forgiveness is and must be an art practiced many times.

We can also learn it, step by step, as we discover that forgiveness is like love. The more we seek to give it to others and to remain open to receiving it, the better able we are to love faithfully and respectfully.

The example and the life of Jesus tell us that if we forgive we shall also be forgiven. And it will not always be easy to forgive. His love and forgiveness was not accepted by unloving and unforgiving enemies. Ours may not be either.

The Rewards of Being a Forgiving Person

One of the classic stories of forgiveness is that of the prodigal son. We usually think of him as being reckless and ungrateful. He demands and receives his inheritance from his father and then wastes it as he destroys a part of his life. Sometime later he returns to his father. He has no money but he has an inner conviction that his father's house is a place of love, a place of unconditional love and forgiveness.

Who of us has not felt like that wastrel of a son as we approach someone we love with a need for forgiveness and with an awareness that we have failed the person again?

Who of us has not sometimes behaved like the elder son of this story, reminding others that we have not failed them and then out of some kind of self-righteous stance we have stripped them of some measure of their self-worth?

Who of us can claim that others can approach us with the same assurance with which the well-travelled younger son approached his father, knowing that they will be embraced and welcomed as he was?

Perhaps we have forgotten that "prodigal" can also mean "one who is extremely generous, even lavish." What son ever offered his father a more lavish gift of love than this son?

What younger brother ever offered an older brother a greater vote of confidence than to return to a home where he would certainly have to deal with the consequences of his decisions?

The life of both sons and the father centers on the tough and tender nature of love and its inherent relationship to forgiveness. We may separate love and forgiveness for purposes of reflection and description, but they are inseparable in fact and in deed.

The seemingly irresponsible choices of the younger son become the occasion for three people who love each other to celebrate the goodness of what they share and to remove some previously unknown obstacles to their ability to grow together in love.

> Forgiveness is the answer to the child's dream of a miracle by which what is broken is made whole again, what is soiled is again made clean. The dream explains why we need to be forgiven, and why we must forgive. In the presence of God, nothing stands between Him and us — we *are* forgiven. But we *cannot* feel His presence if anything is allowed to stand between ourselves and others.
>
> *Markings*, Dag Hammarskjold

8 One Life, Many Gifts

> So many things fail to interest us, simply because they
> don't find in us enough surfaces on which to live, and
> what we have to do is increase the number of planes in
> our mind, so that a much larger number of themes
> can find a plane in it at the same time.
>
> Ortega y Gasset

I love to drive along the Mississippi River in the fall, especially where, through the centuries, it has carved bluffs out of
the sandstone. There I find a stark contrast between the
golden leaves of the elms and aspens, the tan of the box elders
and oaks, the brilliant red of the sugar maples and the green
of the conifers. There is even one small area of apple trees
laden with golden and red apples.

I have hiked through these same woods in spring and
have discovered abundant wild flowers and ferns at the foot of
the trees. Violets and trilliums, bloodroots and dog-toothed
violets, purple and yellow crocuses begin peeking out from
under the accumulation of leaves, pine needles and cones.
Finding a violet or trillium is a nice reward for an afternoon
hike through the woods.

I know of few people who do not notice and enjoy the
natural beauty around them no matter what clime they live
in. Few would deny the goodness of the differences that exist
or the necessity for such variety.

Differences That Enrich and Challenge

Certainly the ocean floor presents a challenge to the deep-sea diver. An arctic explorer must have respect for the icy shapes that surround him. Mountain climbers take precautions against possible trail hazards as they seek the summit. And the captains of the barges that seem to move so easily along the Mississippi respect the powerful forces that can hasten or hinder their progress.

When we begin to consider the differences among races, nationalities and individuals, we enter an entirely different realm. We are forced to deal with the insides of things, with decisions that have to do with values and beliefs, with lifestyles and activities that may somehow affect all of us.

We cherish the differing practical dimensions that are attended to by people who do various tasks within our society: the plumber, the carpenter, the electrician, the fireman, the policeman, the nurse, the teacher, the counsellor. We are neither insecure with nor threatened by people committed to doing practical jobs.

However, if we move beyond the task and reach into the motivations and ideologies of the doer, we come face to face with a person. Once we move beyond what people do to who they are, challenges are immediately more recognizable.

People whose talents differ from ours expand our world. They increase our possibilities of seeing what we have not noticed previously. They call us to move beyond what we know to discover what may seem beyond our reach when we try to do it alone. The more powerful the intersection of lives and gifts, the greater the potential to discover new growing edges and to reach into the unknown regions of our own lives.

The differences we feel between ourselves and others can also activate fears and insecurities never before experienced. Sometimes we feel the desire to run away from the pain that is involved in increasing the number of planes in our minds and hearts. The facets of life reflected through the lives of others may offer life that seems too costly or too threatening to be explored.

We are surprised and disappointed at our lack of openness; we are caught by the fear of moving from where we are into some hitherto unknown place of life. We wonder why the best qualities in another trigger such a perplexing mixture of responses in us.

How many dreams are not fashioned because of such fears? How much creative energy is lost because of inner insecurities which paralyze our spirit of adventure. Even when we may know that the best gifts of another can enrich our lives, we can be overwhelmed and immobilized.

Gifts Not Shared

Along the way, we can be influenced by the ideas and abilities of others in ways that result in new doors being opened or familiar ones closed. Sometimes we are like the little boy in the following story by Helen Buckley which was inspired by Harry Chapin's song, "Flowers Are Red."

One morning,
When a little boy had been in school a while,
The teacher said:
"Today we are going to make a picture."
"Good," thought the little boy.
He liked to make pictures.
He could make all kinds.
Lions and tigers,
Chickens and cows, trains and boats,
And he took out his box of crayons.
And began to draw.
But the teacher said: "Wait!
"It is not time to begin!"

And she waited until everyone looked ready.

"Now," said the teacher,

"We are going to make flowers."

"Good," thought the little boy.

He liked to make flowers,

And he began to make beautiful ones

With his pink and orange and blue crayons.

But the teacher said, "Wait!

"And I will show you how."

And, it was red, with a green stem.

"There," said the teacher,

"Now you may begin."

And the little boy looked at the teacher's flower.

Then he looked at his own.

He liked his flower better.

But he did not say this.

He just turned his paper over

And made a flower just like the teacher's.

It was red with a green stem.

On another day, when the little boy had opened

The door from the outside all by himself,

The teacher said:

"Today we are going to make something with clay."

"Good!" thought the little boy.

He liked clay.

He could make all kinds of things with clay.

Snakes and snowmen,

Elephants and mice, cars and trucks.

And he began to pull and pinch

His ball of clay.
But the teacher said;
"Wait! It is not time to begin!"
And she waited until everyone looked ready.
"Now," said the teacher,
"We are going to make a dish."
He liked to make dishes.
And he began to make some.
They were all shapes and sizes.
But the teacher said, "Wait!
"I will show you how."
And she showed everyone how to make
One deep dish.
"There," said the teacher.
"Now you may begin."
The little boy looked at the teacher's dish,
Then he looked at his own.
He liked his dishes better than the teacher's.
But he did not say this.
He just rolled his clay into a big ball again.
And made a dish like the teacher's.
It was a deep dish.
And pretty soon
The little boy learned to wait,
And to watch
and to make things just like the teacher.
And pretty soon,
He didn't make things of his own anymore.
Then it happened

That the little boy and his family
Moved to another house,
In another city,
And the little boy
Had to go to another school.
And the first day
He was there,
The teacher said:
"Today we are going to make a picture."
"Good," thought the little boy.
And he waited for the teacher
To tell him what to do.
But the teacher didn't say anything.
She just walked around the room,
When she came to the little boy
She said, "Don't you want to make a picture?"
"Yes," said the little boy.
"What are we going to make?"
"I don't know until you make it," said the teacher.
"But how shall I make it?" asked the little boy.
"Why, any way you like," said the teacher.
"And any color?" asked the little boy.
"Any color," said the teacher.
"If everyone makes the same picture,
And used the same colors,
How would I know who made which picture?"
"Why, I don't know," said the little boy.
And then he began to make a red flower with a
    green stem.

When I think about this story, I sometimes see myself as the teacher and sometimes as the little boy. But, in whichever role I place myself, it is clear that we are not always good stewards of our own gifts and we do not always set others free to share their gifts. The greatest gift we can give is to affirm and set free the creativity of others. The greatest tragedy is to not look beyond our own gifts to encourage and rejoice in the abilities of another.

Who Is Responsible for Gifts Not Developed?

The story of the little boy presents some powerful questions: Who is responsible for lost gifts? Who will help discover and recover talents lost or diminished? When and with whom have I been like the over-confident teacher? When and with whom have I been like the little boy? Why do we sometimes lack either the courage or desire to seek the life revealed through ordinary — and sometimes extraordinary — insights into life?

The poet Langston Hughes asks, "What happens to a dream deferred? Does it dry up like a raisin in the sun?" How, why and when are personal dreams deferred? When do we stop dreaming if too many dreams are deferred?

We are a nation born of different races, nationalities, and cultures. We are a people of widely diversified personal histories. Some sought this nation out of a need to be free of oppression. Others were brought here to be oppressed.

We are a church of people with differing expectations and dreams for the fulfillment of Christian values. We are anointed to the sharing of life through our baptism as we seek to discover what it means for us to belong to one another.

We are individuals who seek a personal identity and integrity as we recognize that self-love precedes the gift of self. We long to unlock the secrets of who we are and the gifts that we have to offer. We need to find ways to free those gifts.

Perhaps the questions about who is responsible for lost

gifts need to be recast in a positive note. Perhaps it is better to ask who and what will help us in our rediscovery or recovery process?

Christians believe that God's invitation to life carries with it the reassurance of help in responding. There is more to our lives than ourselves. We can neither plan for nor provide for the presence of people and of circumstances that bring us to greater life. We can only respond to the love of the most magnanimous provider for life.

Part of God's provident love are opportunities never finally lost. There is always another way, a new call, a different way of revealing the same offer of life, the same awareness of the gifts that we have.

But, a part of God's provision of life is that others are a vital part of the process. For every person who has shut some door on us, there is another waiting to open it again. For every person who does not value our gifts, there are others who will and do. For every person who has not encouraged our creative abilities, there are others who will set our energies free by sharing their lives. For every person who did not speak the affirming and life-giving words, there is another who will if we are open to hear and to receive.

The Pain of Sharing Our Gifts

Most of us realize we are set free by those who love us. A less acknowledged truth is that we are also set free by those who differ from us, by those who may not love us. In the presence of someone we are consistently and painfully uncomfortable with, we have an opportunity to discover what it is in us that releases such feelings.

Each of us can identify people who, by sharing their gifts, have set us free to discover and express gifts we may not have known we had. It is a valuable and life-producing reflection to draw our lifeline, indicating all the people along the way who have inspired or challenged us to grow beyond where we were when we met them.

It may be equally valuable and freeing to recall who the people are who have been a part of our lives who seemed to introduce discomfort and self-doubt. It is important to ask the question, "How did it feel and seem then?" "How does it feel and seem now?" Time, well lived, has a way of healing; something viewed in retrospect is usually clearer than it was in foresight.

Who has ever fully comprehended the human chemistry involved in the dynamics of day-to-day meetings which leave people with strong feelings of mutuality and attraction, or of discomfort and rejection? No liberating power in the world is stronger than a meeting for which both people are ready, having been prepared for by all of their lives. And there is no paralyzing force more destructive than the coming together of lives set at odds for reasons neither understand.

If we compare and contrast the effects of such meetings in a somewhat graphic manner, it might look like this:

Positive and freeing	**Negative and limiting**
Greater awareness of my gifts	Questioning of my abilities
Healthy sense of my limitations	A fear that I have only limitations and no strengths
My world is expanded by the vision of another	My world seems threatened by the vision of another
My creative energies are high	I lose a sense of any creative ability
My fears and insecurities are experienced as challenges	I am controlled by my fears and feelings of insecurity
My position is made stronger by the presence of this person in my life	My position feels threatened and limited in this person's presence
My gifts are recognized and affirmed	My gifts seem not to be noticed or affirmed
I have a desire to affirm the other and to recognize that person's gifts	I have a desire to devalue the gifts of another

I have a desire to become more than I presently am	I do not trust my ability to grow and become
I feel at home and safe with this person	I am uncomfortable and untrusting in this person's presence
I feel love being offered	I feel mainly criticism being given

We may lose sight of the fact that the first set of feelings has a comfortable power that supports and sets us free, and the second set introduces into our lives the pain which can call us to new and renewed life. The first we can often accept comfortably, the second is like a reluctant guest who will not leave until we have dealt with the meaning hidden in the encounter.

Reverence: A Gift That Respects All Other Gifts

> And through the grace that I have been given, I say this to every one of you: never pride yourself on being better than you really are . . . all of us, though there are so many of us, make up one body in Christ, and as different parts we are all joined to one another. . . . The gifts that we have differ according to the grace that was given to each of us (Rom 12:3, 5-6).

St. Paul's statement that "we are all joined to one another" is an important basis for our call to cherish one another's gifts and to bear each other's burdens. If we really believe that we stand in that sort of relationship to each other, then we will approach our own gifts with a greater desire to discover and develop them. We will have a greater respect for the talents of others if we gratefully accept our own.

People who are not able to see beyond their own horizons are not likely to see into the treasures hidden in the lives of others. The reverent person approaches the talents of others with a sense of awe and happiness.

People who primarily quest for self-gratification value all things only in terms of their own comfort and immediate satisfaction. The reverent person manifests a thankful and undemanding stance toward life.

People who perceive every good only for their use or possible exploitation will grasp at everything that comes their way regardless of the destruction this may bring. The reverent person carries an innate concern for the life and welfare of all.

People who are intolerant and impatient cannot allow situations and relationships to unfold slowly. Gradually they become the victims of their own restless demands. The reverent person approaches people and things with gentle invitations and cautious care.

People who do not recognize that each of us is enriched and made stronger by the gifts of others may try to diminish either the gift or the possessor. The reverent person who has taken time to reflect on the goodness of life and of the challenge in Paul's words seeks to understand more fully what it means for us to belong to one another.

People who do not believe things are good and beautiful and worthwhile in and of themselves often demand that everything must somehow stand in relationship to them and to their needs. The reverent person believes that people and things have value simply because they are.

People who are overly concerned with their own good name and their ability to exercise influence over others become slaves of their desire for reputation. The reverent person learns to value who he or she is and can become.

People who have never taken time or energy to seek the meaning hidden in their failures, their limitations, their broken relationships, their unwillingness to accept or offer forgiveness will have been frustrated in their suffering and blinded by their pain. The reverent person has taken time and made the effort to uncover the beauty of the human condition and the meaning hidden in human suffering.

People who believe that they can control people and events will miss no opportunity to place themselves in the position of power and to keep that position at whatever cost. The reverent person knows the experience and remembers well the hard-earned lesson that every life has periods of powerlessness and times when we are not in control. The reverent person has come to accept the truth that life will eventually break us and destroy us unless we learn the important and humanizing lesson of being powerless.

Reverence is a gentle virtue; it is also strong. Reverence is a tender virtue; it is also tough. Reverence is a patient virtue; it is also persistent. Reverence bears no ill will toward others; it is able to bear the ill will of others when necessary. Reverence is a virtue that prepares us well to belong to one another; it reaches out to those who have given messages of not wishing to belong.

When we approach others with gentle reverence, we bring the hope-filled expectation that they will respond to our gifts and share theirs with us.

9 *Life at the Center*

At the still point of the turning world. Neither flesh
　　nor fleshless;
Neither from nor towards; at the still point, there the
　　dance is
But neither arrest nor movement. And do not call it
　　fixity,
Where past and future are gathered. Neither move-
　　ment from nor towards
Neither ascent nor decline. Except for the point, the
　　still point
There would be no dance . . .

Burnt Norton, T.S. Eliot

Whatever life we discover at the margins must be verified and tested at the center. What we first become aware of at the margins is like an indicator pointing toward the center. The closer we seek to come toward the center, the more we realize the unplumbed depths of our lives. The more we recognize that the journey to the precious still point will never end, the more we become aware that it is as rewarding as it is fraught with profound pain. As we invest in discovering that central place, we realize that the still point is always moving.

If we have savored, however slightly, that place of life, we have surely discovered that the journey there can never be made alone. Its nature and fruitfulness can be realized only in the companionship of others. We were never meant to dance alone. The greatest meaning in the dance is in sharing it. Human intimacy is a constitutive dimension of the rewarding

129

search for the center which yields up the still point as a fitting reward for our faithful and demanding quest.

Every person needs intimacy; it is not one of life's luxuries. Even if we could make the journey alone, it would have no meaning. Life must be shared. The greater the depth of the living, the more intense is our need to share it, and the greater is our vulnerability. We risk all in this venture.

Intimacy is like the pearl of great price which, as the gospel tells us, was purchased with a lifetime's savings. If we value intimacy above the ability to sustain many superficial relationships, we are into a high risk adventure.

Morris West recounts an insightful incident in the biography of Carl Jung, *The World Is Made of Glass:*

Jung and a woman friend are discussing her visit to a place in the Orient where jewels are bought and sold. She tells Jung of her visit to a small village where she is taught to read stones: the silk in an emerald, the luster of pearls and the depth of color in a ruby. Because this is a place which deals especially in pearls, she is introduced to a man who is a pearl peeler.

The man explains that a pearl is formed of many layers of nacre which the oyster deposits over an irritant, usually sand, in its shell. He tells her that even fine pearls sometimes have defects in their outer skins: pinhole pittings, tiny indented marks on the surface. If these marks are not too deep, they can be removed by peeling away the layers of nacre until a perfect layer is reached.

This man claims his work is an art, delicate and sometimes costly, for the jewel can be destroyed. Merchants who buy pearls must bid on them after they have examined the jewel but before the pearl peeler begins. The pearl peeler holds a handful of pearls for the woman to look at, and then says of the merchants, "It takes a lot of nerve to bid blind on the ultimate value of a pearl."

Intimacy: Bidding Blind on the Still Point

Even the best informed and studied of bidders is still a gambler. He has no way of knowing what lies beyond what he can see. So it is with intimacy. We have no way of knowing what lies in our undiscovered regions; neither does a person we choose as an important companion. We have no certain evidence that the effort we invest will be returned with proportionate growth for ourselves and for the one with whom we seek the center.

Our approach to that moving still point is affected by a set of inner attitudes and outer obstacles. The ultimate value of the intimacy we seek is reflected to us through the questions we ask about it and through our willingness to share all of this with our companion.

Is intimacy a gift or a reward?

A reward is usually looked upon as something given in exchange for an act of service or merit. We expect the reward if we fulfill the requirements. If we approach intimacy this way we will expect to receive it. There is a clarity about it. We give this and, in exchange, receive something we desire.

But a gift is something given; there is no exchange. We can develop the proper attitudes in ourselves which prepare us to receive the gift another may offer. If we consider intimacy a gift, then we will be concerned about removing the barriers in ourselves which make us reluctant receivers. Our motivation is to be open to all of life, not to expect to receive some specific thing.

Receiving a reward has to do with outer actions; openness to receive a gift is related to inner attitudes. We can be deserving of a reward but never of a gift.

Can we have intimacy, or must we continually seek it?

If intimacy is something we have, then we approach it as something attainable. We approach it as a project that we can complete and then enjoy.

If intimacy is something we seek, then a part of its value is in the seeking. We perceive it as an unfolding reality which we can approach but never totally possess. We approach it as a value rather than as a thing.

Having something implies certainty; seeking something implies having no guarantees. To speak of having intimacy implies completion; to speak of being intimate reflects more accurately a life-giving approach to it.

Does it begin with another or with myself?

In its Latin root word, intimate literally implies the necessity to be as close inside ourselves as we can be. It begins inside, but it cannot remain there.

Intimacy is what I like to call an "inside out process." We reach out to another because of something within us; ideally, the other person does the same thing. Then, after sharing and exchanging whatever we can, we reach back into ourselves to some slightly deeper place so that we have more to share in our next interchange.

The nature of the process is such that it must begin in each but cannot end there. The inner and outward movements are inseparable. By the very nature of the process, it is both inner- and outer-directed.

What is the role of solitude in intimacy?

Intimacy also implies the need for ongoing efforts toward self-discovery and self-love, both of which require quiet time and space.

Intimacy is impossible for two people if either or both give themselves away in the relationship. Presence to self is not likely to be a value if self-worth is in question.

The firmer the relationship each has with self, the stronger the ground on which the relationship can grow. Rainer Maria Rilke says that for love to grow, two solitudes must "meet and protect and cherish one another." When two strong and separate selves stand in relationship to one another, the gifts of each become clearer and grow stronger. The entire process is nourished in and through solitude.

No amount of questioning about the nature of intimacy can be allowed to replace a firm commitment to its beauty and value. Like the pearl buyers, we bid blind, knowing neither the total cost nor the possibilities of the hidden treasure.

Intimacy: The Process of Transformation

By our nature, we are called to be self-reflective and inner-directed. We are also challenged to share the journey and to be other-directed. To live with these values is to be in a place of tension. In this tension we will not be harmed if we see them as working together to produce new life. In the place of the tension is also to be found the place of transformation.

In the book of Ezekiel we read:

> For I shall take you from among the nations and gather you back from all the countries, and bring you home to your own country. I shall pour clean water over you and you will be cleansed; I shall cleanse you of all your filth and of all your foul idols. I shall give you a new heart, and put a new spirit in you; I shall remove the heart of stone from your bodies and give you a heart of flesh instead (Ez 36:24-26).

Through self-reflection, we come home to our own land; we open ourselves to inner-direction; we are cleansed and prepared to receive the gift of a new heart, a heart set free of obstacles and exorcized of inner idols, now freed of its inflexibilities and self-centeredness.

But the transformation of the human heart does not happen merely by wishing it. Neither is it simply the result of words we say or of actions we perform. Like the layers of nacre that must be removed flake by flake, layer by layer, so do we carry accretions which must be removed.

We must free ourselves of the false notion of community which allows us to believe that we can love races and groups.

Love does not begin in public and in groups. It begins in solitude and in relationship to self. Nourished by solitude and
prepared by a good relationship to self, we reach out to a person. We do not love in bunches or in groups; we love one to
one. Groups first come to be interconnected by the bonds that
unite one person to another and another and another. If we
seek to love nations out of some voiced concern for the world,
we may lose the world we have. If we have the courage to pay
the high price that a long-term relationship inevitably asks of
us, we have a starting place from which to build world community.

Jesus is a good role model for us. The more he became
involved in his public life the more he needed to go apart to
pray and to listen carefully for Yahweh's call. The support of
his public life came from that group he gathered most closely
around him. Even among those few, some were closer to the
center than others.

Gandhi often used to say, "For the sake of the people of
India I must sometimes withdraw from them and from public
life so that I might return after being nourished and renewed
in strength."

We must free ourselves from the automatic associations
we sometimes make between intimacy and sexuality. In our
time of permissiveness and reduced respect for the power and
the goodness of all that is genuinely sexual, we must see intimacy as much more inclusive than just bodies coming together. Easy sexual expression is robbed of its meaning and
beauty unless there is a mutual commitment to the costly and
difficult process of all that is involved in the quest for intimacy.

To believe that the only intimacy that matters for us is to
be found in relationships with persons of the opposite sex is
also limiting and destructive. Every person has gifts to offer,
every person makes our world. If Pozzo in *Waiting for Godot*
could say, "Every person brings something to my life; from
even the meanest creature, I depart a richer and wiser man,"

then we might free ourselves from the error of too easily concluding that someone has nothing to offer to our lives.

We are sometimes guilty of projections that have more to do with our own frailty and insecurity than that of another. Subconsciously, we sometimes react against qualities that we either see or think we see in another when, in reality, we are reacting to something in ourselves. Growth in self-knowledge and self-understanding can begin to free us from the possible harm we do to ourselves and others when we strike out in this way.

Our understanding of the meaning of intimacy and relationship first began for us in our own families. From infancy on we have inherited patterns of behavior related to what we observed going on around us. For some of us, the family of origin was a place that prepared us well with a deposit of good relational skills and with some sense of the goodness and beauty of intimate sharing. For some of us, little or none of this was present. To accept the present and to give direction to the future, we may need to delve into our past and to free ourselves of behavior that can obstruct or destroy intimacy.

We need to be aware of the impact of the cultural influences that surround us and get inside us. We need some convictions about the irrevocable harm that will be done to the human race if we come to value technology over intimacy, affluence over the riches of the human heart. As Needleman writes in *The Way of the Physician*:

> New technologies constantly infiltrate my life like painted whores. They give me powers I never dreamt of and lure me away from the feeling of myself, by which feeling alone a man can live his life like a man. I confront the obligations of a man without the feelings of a man. And therefore I am bewildered by all the new knowledge being served up to us in this new world we are all entering.

Needleman's reflections are as much a call to transformation as are the words of Ezekiel. Ezekiel speaks of coming home from foreign countries and Needleman questions the foreign land of technology. Both speak of the need to tend to our hearts. Each presents a challenge to respond to what is of and for life and to flee from whatever outside forces would interfere with who we are and who we can become.

The transformation that begins and ends in each person's heart touches the hearts of others. The quest for intimacy is related to and serves as the basis for the wider community which is the family, the neighborhood, the nation and the world.

Intimacy: Experiences of Darkness and Light

When we ask the questions "What kind of life do I want?" and "Where do I want my life to be centered?," we may recognize what has interfered with our quest for intimacy. These questions may help us give new direction to our lives. We may find patterns we have gravitated toward and not understand why. We may notice the contrasts in the places where we have looked for life or hidden from it.

The security of the margins

Sometimes, because we have been hurt or afraid of being hurt, we make careful choices that will allow us to stay a safe distance from someone we say we care about. We remain marginal to whatever possibilities might exist in growing closer.

For a while we may not even be aware that we are keeping the place between us. We seek the lifeless security of sharing only a little of who we are, perhaps just enough to still claim even the weakest of bonds.

In relationships, we receive in proportion to our investment of ourselves. If security is a greater value than intimacy, we cannot place the blame outside ourselves for the quality of life we are able to share.

The comfort of the middle ground

While we might carefully avoid being marginal to a relationship, we might persuade ourselves that we have been faithful if we take a few, carefully guarded steps closer. When we do this, we may initially be well rewarded. With each small step we may reap the excitement of some small increment of growth shared with another. The other person may reinforce the value of these reluctant steps in the name of sensitivity or gentleness.

Though limited movement in mutual growth is enriching and life-giving it will not, in the end, sustain the friendship. To set limits on the possible life that could be realized is to initiate the beginning of its destruction.

We are called to love without limit, to care without measuring, and, sometimes, to experience the pain of growth without regretting. There is no comfortable way to reach the center where intimacy is rewarded.

The costly life at the center

By reason of our baptism, we are called to the life at the center. When we are anointed with the sacred chrism, we are committed to sharing life with others. Together we are committed as Christians to seek life to the full, God's promise to us. Such life will not be found at the margins. We may taste a little of it in the comfort of the middle ground. But, only at the center will we experience the goodness and beauty of life's richest gifts. Only at the center will we know that the price of intimacy is continually being rewarded. Only when we know what the presence of another person can mean, only then can we look back with gratitude.

From a different point of view, we might say that to choose either the margins or the middle ultimately costs us all and offers no lasting rewards.

Robert Frost speaks of the still point as "an inside in" place:

Listen and I will take my dearest risk.
We're always too much out or too much in.
At present we're so much out that the odds are
    against
Our ever getting inside in again.
But inside in is where we've got to get.

He also speaks of it as a place of highest, dearest risk. A place so sacred and so difficult to reach that only a person with a bit of a gambler's soul would attempt it. Only a person willing to walk in darkness for the sake of the possible light will set out on and be faithful to the journey.

Our own experience and that of others tell us that

— The quest for intimacy will sometimes lead into the heart of darkness.
— The quest for intimacy will sometimes exact the pain-filled tears that cleanse and heal.
— The quest for intimacy will lead us into the blinding light of self-truth that is as precious as it is terrifying.
— The quest for intimacy will sometimes involve us in doubting our ability to make so costly a commitment.
— The quest for intimacy will sometimes challenge us to be more present to, and more patient with ourselves.
— The quest for intimacy will sometimes remind us of past mistakes in relationships and call us to avoid hurting ourselves or another.
— The quest for intimacy will sometimes find us weary and faltering as we wonder why the ways of love are so demanding.
— The quest for intimacy will sometimes be so pain-filled that we will realize that no other life venture has been so powerful a teacher.

The value of the journey is recognized, and the suffering along the way is rewarded with many gifts that we would attain in a lesser degree, if at all, if we pursued another way. The shared darkness and difficulty that lead to the still point is a process in which lives are bonded in a way possible along no other path.

We may look for easier ways to grow in self-knowledge and self-love, but there are none. We may hope for less complicated decisions as we deal with our own complexity and that of another, but there are none. We may expect to realize more of the rewards of our efforts all along the way, but it may not be possible. The rewards of valuing intimacy are in the long-distance run and not in the short-term commitment. The fulfillment of God's promise is fulfilled only at the center of life.

The life shared at the center, the reward of the passage from darkness to light, is well described in John's gospel:

> What has come into being in him was life,
> life that was the light of men;
> and light shines in darkness,
> and darkness could not overpower it (Jn 1:4-5).

Strangers Walking in Darkness No Longer

One of the most rewarding and challenging prerequisites for the journey to the still point is the desire to know ourselves. Unless we have been faithful to the process of self-discovery, there can be no self-giving. To know and cherish ourselves is where we begin to cherish another.

Our culture does not provide strong support for the self-involvement required to be intimate. Rather it glamorizes the casual and impersonal involvement of bodies, and makes excuses for irresponsible and exploitative encounters. Just as we can learn powerful lessons from the beauty of relationships, so too can we gain insights through mutually destructive relationships. Witnessing violence that is named love, and exploitations called involvement, we can become more aware of our own rationalizations and our own carelessness in approaching the sacred space of another.

Henrik Ibsen, in his powerful play *A Doll's House,* portrays very profoundly the story of an eight-year marriage. On the surface of things the relationship between Nora and Torvald might appear ideal.

Nora is a meticulous keeper of the house and a welcoming hostess offering flawless hospitality. Torvald tells Nora that she has loved him as any good woman ought to love her husband. But, as he continues, he reveals the insides of their relationship. Nora, according to Torvald's description, is a woman who does not understand how to act on her own responsibility. He says, "No, no, lean on me; I will advise and direct you." He goes on to say that her very attractiveness to him is her helplessness.

Nora has been aware that their marriage has not been a place of loving intimacy but of destructive dependence that Torvald demands in the name of love.

When she tells him the truth that she sees, his response is, "Let me help you if you are in want."

Nora's final words to Torvald describe what happens when people who give public witness to sharing their lives either have not learned or have not been willing to pay the price for moving from the security of the margins.

When Torvald offers again to allow her to lean on him, he is stunned by the power of her decisive and self-liberating words. Her response allows nothing more. She says simply, "No. I can receive nothing from a stranger."

Nora and Torvald had done violence to themselves and to one another through their lack of commitment to a deeply shared life. We are relational people, men and women who cannot grow and will certainly not reach the fullness of life without involving ourselves in the journey to the center.

If we enter a relationship only superficially, we shall reap only a small reward, if any. If we are willing to root out the obstacles we will greatly increase our benefits. If we pay the dearest price for the most costly and most rewarding choice, the decision to plunge into the deepest regions of life, we will not easily again be a stranger to ourselves or to another.

10 *Growing Strong at Broken Places*

Life breaks us all sometimes, but some grow strong at broken places.

Ernest Hemingway

For most people pain and suffering are associated with bodily hurts. We think of hospital emergency rooms and accident victims; hospices and long-term cancer victims waiting to die; burn centers and children waiting for another skin graft. We read about families who have a loved one afflicted with Alzheimer's disease. We hear about the increase in the number of AIDS victims and the frightened responses of their families and friends.

Support systems of all kinds are formed to help the physically sick and those whose lives are affected. It is well recognized that the family that gives love and care also needs to be loved and cared for — the healthy need to be healed of a different kind of hurt.

Every person alive has felt some physical pain. No one grows up without having had hurts that brought tears that needed to be kissed away by someone who cared. Every person has fallen down and scraped a knee, cut a finger, needed stitches, had a sore throat or suffered some childhood illness.

We have read and heard the stories of people who learned to walk again when they were told that they could not. We know stories of people who survived the most serious injuries or heart attacks against all the predictions of others. We admire both their stamina and their desire to live. We listen and we learn about pain.

Pain: Immeasurable or Unmeasurable?

Caring people respond with manifest concern to the physical suffering of others. Good people hurt inside when they come close to the hurting of another. Most of us grew up simply believing that caring about someone in pain is the decent thing to do.

If we reflect on situations we have observed, we know that our initial interest and response is sometimes not sustained. We move on to another concern. We sometimes forget about the person for whom the physical hurt is a constant and long-term companion.

One summer when I was attending school, I used to see a young man named Jim every morning as I walked along the river. He was in a wheelchair, paralyzed from the waist down. He had been injured when he dove into a mountain lake without realizing that the water level had been greatly lowered by a nearby dam.

Several times each day he would go to this place where I would see him. He would lift himself out of his wheelchair by grasping at a heavy rope which a friend had secured on one branch of a huge tree. He told me that every movement of every muscle hurt but that he was determined to regain the use of his legs. With tears in his eyes he said, "Friends were there for me when the accident first happened. My hospital room was filled with flowers and gifts. Now, I don't see much of my friends. You know how it is, their lives have to go on."

Living alone in an apartment, continuing work on a degree in chemical engineering, and hoping to keep the love of his fiancée seemed to me a nearly overwhelming project for one young man. His friends did not understand that he still needed them and, typical of his age and ability, he was not used to asking for help.

Physical pain has an elusive quality. Even dedicated doctors have no way of measuring or accurately describing the pain a patient feels. There is no way of comparing the pain of two people suffering with the same kind of affliction.

We hear about differing thresholds. We read that some people have a greater tolerance than others. Nurses describe the differences they see in patients, some of whom demand pain-relieving medication and others of whom refuse to take that same medication.

A woman who has suffered from rheumatoid arthritis for more than 50 years showed me her gnarled fingers and her nearly unrecognizable toes. I had never seen such distortion and just looking at her hands and feet evoked a deep emotional response. This gentle, beautiful woman said, "I cannot remember when I did not hurt."

There is no way to compare her suffering with that of a 10-year-old boy left hairless from radiation therapy. And there is no need to try to. For each, and for their families, the suffering is both unmeasured and immeasurable.

Physical Pain and Inward Suffering

Whether we speak of psychosomatic illness or wholistic healing, we are reminded that body and inner spirit are linked to one another in such a way that what affects one will affect the other. The hurts of the heart can have profound implications for the functioning of the body. The wounds sustained as we dedicate ourselves to the inward journey are sure to tap the resources of energy needed for the outer activities of life.

Terms like mental illness and physical suffering may give some indication of where the illness is rooted but never that it is restricted to either the body or the psyche. Physical suffering may be located in some specific area or system of the body while mental anguish is felt in one's whole being. Yet, one single aching tooth seems to fill the entire body with pain.

Recently a woman who has been committed to psychiatric wards several times told me that she would rather have cancer or coronary disease than mental illness because, as she said, "When people are on the cancer floor, the attitude of others is one of compassion. It's not like being judged wacko."

None of us can or dare make comparisons between our hurts and those of another, magnifying ours and minimizing another's. It is a very human thing to be overly aware of the pain in our life and the happiness in the life of another. Suffering is unique and sacred in its possibilities for greater life for each person who experiences the pain. Our pain reminds us of our call as human companions to reverence one another's gifts, one of which is our unique suffering. If, as St. Paul says, "We belong to one another," then his words in 1 Corinthians have added meaning as we recognize the differing faces of suffering:

> . . . God has put all the separate parts into the body as he chose. If they were all the same part, how could it be a body? As it is, the parts are many but the body is one. The eye cannot say to the hand, "I have no need of you," and nor can the head say to the feet, "I have no need of you."
>
> What is more, it is precisely the parts of the body that seem to be the weakest which are the indispensable ones (1 Cor 12:18-22).

Some Guides Leading Us to the Giftedness of Pain

No book on suffering would be complete without including something on physical pain. But as I look to myself and to the members of my immediate family, I realize that I have not had any real experience with physical pain. For such a great blessing I am deeply grateful; because of this same blessing, I am also limited in my understanding of and closeness to physical pain.

For this reason and others, I have asked people who have known physical pain or who have been close to it to give some personal testimony as to what that pain meant to them, how they coped with it, and what it has brought into their lives. The stories are theirs.

Mary: A child of poverty and polio

Some of my earliest childhood memories are of being picked up by the police and carried home. You see, my father was an alcoholic and, even at age 3 or 4, I figured out that if I went to the bars with him I might be able to help him get home safely. So, when my father went into the tavern to drink, I would sit down in the doorway to wait for him. Sometimes when my father would leave the tavern drunk, he would forget that I had come with him. By that time, I might have fallen asleep and would later be found by the police who took me home.

My father died when I was five. I don't remember much about his death except that I knew that we loved each other. I did not feel that way about my mother and brother and sister. And, when it was time for me to go to school, they did not want me to go. Somehow, even then, I was somewhat of a fighter and so I went anyway.

We were very poor and the little shack we lived in was isolated from the rest of the town. The first day that I went to school, I went barefoot. I did not know that other children wore shoes to school.

I stayed in school, though my brother and sister who had never gone became even more hateful to me. Then, when I was 11 I got very sick. I remember lying in the bed that all three of us slept in, not able to move. When I heard my mother say, "I think Mary is dead," I was very frightened they might just bury me.

I was able to just move my hand, so my mother knew that I was alive. Now I know that I had polio. I was hospitalized and was the happiest I had ever been when I was there.

My story would be much too long if I were to tell all of it, but, I did recover from polio and I did finish school. With the help of a scholarship, I was able to leave a very miserable home to go to college. I became a teacher and have had a good life.

Then, six years ago, the polio recurred. I could not speak and my vocal chords had to be replaced. I was determined to recover so that I could speak again and return to teaching. I was able to do that.

Beyond the pain of the polio, both when I was young and more recently, was the misery of a filthy home and a family that I now know were all emotionally ill. What kept me going through all of it was the memory of an alcoholic father who, sick though he was, did hold me and love me and care for me. He told me that he wanted things for me that he had never had for himself.

The scholarship which freed me from a destructive and unloving family and the help of a couple of teachers who encouraged me to stay in school now leaves me with the hope that I might still be able to do something for my mother and brother and sister.

I am teaching in an inner-city school. All the children who are in that school live in ghetto homes. Some have loving families, but many do not. The great gift of having survived polio twice is that I know that I have something to offer that others do not. My pain has been richly rewarded. Even if I can never help make the life of my mother and brother and sister better, I believe that my pain has made me a better person and that I can do things for others that my father said he wanted to do for me.

The fragile dreams of a champion skier

My husband and I were high school sweethearts. We met as members of the ski team. Because we were both good skiers, we had lots of opportunities to improve our abilities. I made the junior olympics. My dream was to become a member of the Olympic team, a dream never realized.

We were married when we were very young. Neither of us went on to college. A few years after we were married, I began having mysterious pain and aching legs and arms. Our ski trips became less frequent. After some time we discovered that I had rheumatoid arthritis.

Through the many years since then, the disease has progressed and the pain has increased, nearly crippling me at times. I have been afraid of what this would do to my husband. I wondered if he would leave me, if he would be willing to share the rest of his life with an invalid.

Several times, I contemplated suicide as the solution to my problems and my husband's burden of a wife who has not always dealt well with the pain. It often seemed to me that my death would make it easier for both of us.

I have not taken my own life and my husband has continued to share his life with me and has continued to love me. I do not know how we would have had the courage to do this had not my often immobile body led me to study and love the natural beauty around me. Because our home was in a beautiful natural setting, I could watch the birds who came to our well-stocked feeders and observe the small animals who lived in the woods.

I learned bird calls and began to paint what I could see outside my windows. The beauty around me somehow got inside me and I had a desire to save this beauty by putting it on small pieces of wood and on canvas.

On some days my fingers hurt too much to hold even the smallest paintbrush but, when I could not record what I saw with my brush, I still heard the lovely songs of the birds at the feeders.

How grateful I am that I was not so afraid of pain to choose to feel nothing ever again. I would never have known the wondrous beauty around me and, much more, I would never have received the gift of more than 30 years of faithful love of a good man who was not afraid of his own pain.

Injured at 14, still hurting at 20

My father was a construction worker. I hardly knew him, even though I was his only son. We never did the things together that many of my friends did with their fathers.

One day when I was 14, my father was working in our

garage with a torch. The fuel tank exploded, killing him. I was burned all over my body. I do not remember much about that day except my mother crying and the ambulance coming.

I do remember well the weeks that followed. The doctor told me that 75% of my body was burned and that, if I lived, I would have years of reconstructive plastic surgery ahead of me.

I also remember how ashamed I was because it hurt so much that I would cry and scream. There was no way I could turn, no position that they could put me in that didn't bring tears to my eyes. It didn't even help a lot when my favorite nurse told me that burns like mine hurt more than any other kind of injury. I used to ask her if it would ever stop hurting, if the pain would ever be less. Last year I was so discouraged that I tried to commit suicide.

I am 20 now and am still not finished with surgery. My body doesn't hurt now, except sometimes after surgery. I wonder what the future holds for me. I just want to live a normal life like other guys my age. I want to love someone and have a family. Sometimes I wonder if I can ever find a way to help other kids who get burned. Maybe some of my nurses can help me do that.

The discomfort of others with my pain

I was on my way home from work one evening. I did not look carefully enough at a busy intersection and I was knocked down by a car as it turned off from a busy thoroughfare. I was unconscious and taken to the emergency room of a nearby hospital.

When I regained consciousness, I discovered that my hospital bed resembled a cage. I had a broken leg in traction. I had a broken arm suspended in a sling. Because of a head injury, there was a pin through my skull holding my head so that I could not turn it. And, my jaw was wired shut. I was being fed intravenously, and my only way of communicating with the nurses was by writing on a clipboard which they would hold.

Two friends came to visit soon after the accident. I had one of them hold the clipboard so that I might tell them how I was feeling and also answer their questions.

One was so uncomfortable with the sight of me that when I had written my first message, she quickly took the pen and began to write a note. As I pointed to my ears and smiled, another person with her said, "She is trying to tell you that there isn't anything wrong with her ears. She can hear and see, she just can't talk."

This happened more than once. It reminded me that, however much my body hurt all over, some of the people who came to see me had their own kind of pain and discomfort with how I looked and with the tubes and pins and slings that kept me alive. Some were afraid to touch me or to kiss me goodbye when they left.

The pain and joy of bringing new life into the world

Being a certified nurse-midwife for over 10 years to thousands of laboring women, and having birthed three of my own in that time, childbirth pain is something I feel almost daily. Although many times in jest I proclaim that if I were the creator, childbirth would have been designed quicker, easier, and pain-free, I have come to respect and accept this pain.

Fortunately, gone are the days when a woman had to bear her pain of labor alone in a room, biting a wooden spoon, unaware and fearful of what was happening. Advances in medicine and childbirth education have made things more humane, but have also added confusing messages. Some well-intentioned childbirth educators, by carefully choosing the words labor contractions, rushes, and tightenings as substitutes for the word "pain," have done a great injustice. Are they suggesting that by denying the word, childbirth will occur without pain? Many women are angry after their deliveries because of the false expectations they were led to hold. Did they somehow fail because they had experienced downright pain? Analgesics and anesthetics are improving to maximize levels of pain relief while attempting to minimize deleterious effects to the fetus and labor progress.

But is childbirth pain so inherently bad that we should work to alleviate that completely? One client, after having her first baby "natural," had her second baby with epidural anesthesia as soon as she reached the labor unit. Now expecting her third baby, she had decided that she didn't want the block this time. She had felt more detached from her entire second childbirth and felt that somehow she had missed much of the experience. She stated she didn't feel she could claim it as her own saying, "The doctor delivered my second baby. I want to give birth to my third."

Although admittedly simplistic, I see women having two basic personal approaches to their childbirth experiences. One approach is a passive one in which a woman sees herself as the victim of what must happen in order to have the baby born. The childbirth process is beyond her control. She welcomes the medical professionals who will rescue her from this plight, this painful experience. She resists suggestions to begin taking an active part in her own labor. She essentially denies that pain should enter her life, choosing to escape it as totally as possible. And, when the labor is over, she tends to apologize, embarrassed about her loud noises and reactions to the pain and to thank everyone for "delivering" her baby.

The other approach to the pain of childbirth is an active one. Here the woman sees herself as the one who is going to give birth to her child. She takes ownership of the experience. With her health professionals, she prepares and learns what she needs to do to endure the accompanying delivery pain and enhance the laboring process. She is aware that she is her best health provider and carer. By claiming this responsibility, she is ready to claim the added responsibility of "carer" for her child.

Although this woman does not enjoy pain, she is aware of what the pain is. Instead of resisting her contractions, by letting them come, peak, and fade, she is able to better relax. She will tend to walk (dance) or groan (sing) with her contractions, participating actively in the process. "Yes, let's try this." "No, I'd rather do this right now." Decisions are made together. She may appear to others as bossy or unappreciative, but really, she is birthing and needs to give it her whole being.

The pain she experiences is real. I believe birth is a time in most of our lives when we feel vulnerable and close to our own deaths. The pain can be so overwhelming and it keeps on coming. Will we be able to continue? Will it be better? Will it be worse? It is so much more powerful than anything else we experience in our day-to-day lives, and yet, somehow it does end. We reach down, surprised that there is still any strength there at all, and we pull our babies up to our breast, embracing them in our waiting arms, meeting them, loving them. Tears come. Are we still alive? We did it! We accepted our vulnerability. We claimed this childbirth — we endured it. And somehow, nothing in our lives will ever be the same again. We are victorious! No apologies about anything are needed. Look what we have done! Isn't it wonderful?

Some Universal Elements in Physical Suffering

The stories of others reveal some common elements about bodily suffering.

There is a uniquely personal quality about pain. It belongs primarily to the person experiencing it. No comparisons are possible; none would be helpful. Even two people with the same diagnosis would be vastly different in their attitude and response; each would describe the pain differently.

There is a disruptive dimension to illness. Life's plan cannot go on as intended while pain claims our attention and energy. Significant physical suffering is an all-encompassing, all-involving presence.

There is a form of loneliness that is related to illness. The one who suffers knows that just as no one else can do the suffering for her, so also, no one else can know just how it feels. Verbal descriptions, whether to doctor, nurse or friend, are never adequate to convey the truth of what the pain means to the one who hurts. And, if the illness is long, friends who were faithful to visits and messages of care in the beginning may forget what the one who suffers cannot.

People respond in very different ways to the presence of pain. Some seek to escape it immediately, others are more patient. Some are angry at the intrusion of so unwelcome a companion. Others set about to penetrate the mystery of suffering in an effort to find meaning for their lives. Some grow more beautiful and loving, others become embittered. Some discover God's presence in their lives, others refuse to believe in God's loving care. Some choose self-determination, others choose self-pity.

These and other responses remind us that if, like Job, we ask, "Why must I suffer?" we will give vast amounts of energy to an unanswerable question. If, instead, we ask, "How am I suffering?" we will enter into a sacred journey where God's love will be found in the new life that will be given us.

11 Heartsight: The Gift We Seek

> . . . There is another physical law that teases me, too:
> the Doppler Effect. The sound of anything coming at
> you — a train, say, or the future — has a higher pitch
> than the sound of the same thing going away. . . .
> I would like to hear your life as you heard it, coming
> at you, instead of hearing it as I do, a sober sound of
> expectations reduced, desires blunted, hopes deferred
> or abandoned, chances lost, defeats accepted, griefs
> borne. I don't find your life uninteresting, as Rodman
> does. I would like to hear it as it sounded while it was
> passing.
>
> *Angle of Repose,* Wallace Stegner

The Talmud reminds its readers that "An unexamined life is like an unopened letter." St. Paul encouraged the early Christians to be self-reflective when he said, "be very careful about the sort of lives you lead" (Eph 5:15). And Socrates taught his followers that "the unexamined life is not worth living."

Jesus called to accountability those who had well-functioning ears, yet refused to listen and hear; he rebuked those who had the gift of vision, yet refused to see.

It is not the man born blind who deserves our pity, but the one who sees and refuses to respond to what he sees. It is not the deaf person who carries our deepest concern, but the one who will not listen to the truth of life.

Since the beginning of time, men and women have made the journey along new and potentially dangerous roads strengthened by the vision of a life they sought for themselves and those they loved. Men and women have followed calls to greater life based only on the insights they received from inner resources. None had well-defined road maps and none had absolute certainty that their goal could be realized.

Sometimes the journey to discover greater life emerges out of a frightened sense of being lost; sometimes out of the joy of being finally found again.

This journey has a threefold dimension: We must be awake so that we notice life as it approaches; we must reflect on its meaning after it passes; and out of these, we must try to give direction to life's future.

Seeing and hearing are not enough. If our desire is the fullest life, we must make the effort to see into, to listen into. Only when we have first seen, and then seen into can we hope to see outward—from the inside out. Only then can we hope to respond to what we have heard from what resounds from deep within us.

Some Young Teachers Who Saw and Heard

We usually look to the old for wisdom. We expect that years of experience will bring insight. Sometimes we forget or fail to notice that the young, whose vision has not yet been clouded with prejudice or laden with unrealistic expectations, may yet have an uncluttered vision. They may have an ability to hear the subtleties of life that are both precious and practical. What a tragic loss if these gifts are not sometimes acknowledged and explored.

Jenny: Blind from the time of birth.

I can still remember how terrified I was when Jenny came into my chemistry lab, white cane in one hand and guitar case in the other. I had never before taught a blind student in a chemistry class and had taught only one other person who was blind.

I wondered if I ought to ask her to reconsider her choice of chemistry. The potential dangers seemed alarming. I wondered what student I might select as a lab partner for her.

My initial insecurities gave way to open and much more relaxed attitudes. I quickly discovered that her interest and motivation were significantly greater than that of many of the other students in that same class. She spoke of seeing reactions with a tone that nearly persuaded me she had actually been healed of her blindness.

Though Jenny was new to our high school, before long she was elected to positions of student leadership. She was a member of the debate team, the special vocal group and the drama club. She was loved by the other students and she let them know that she needed no favors.

I smile now as I remember how she and her father came to school one night to get Jenny's special typewriter. As I let them in the front entrance her father and I stopped to visit. When I noticed that she was about to go up the stairs, I excused myself to her father saying, "Just a moment, let me turn on some lights for her." Her father smiled, put a gently restraining hand on my arm, and said, "I don't think Jenny will know that the lights are not on."

I later learned that she had been blinded at birth because of excessive oxygen use. In their disappointment, her parents sought special courses so they could help her live a normal life. Her mother told me that one of the nurse's at the hospital told them, "Jenny was born blind. Please, don't make her a dependent cripple. Do not do anything for her that she can and ought to do for herself."

When I knew Jenny better, I told her about how I had felt when she came into my lab the first day. I asked her how being blind had felt, how she had learned to deal with it, and who had helped her.

She told me that as a little girl she used to run home to cry when the other kids didn't want her to play with them because she couldn't do all the things they could. She said that she was afraid that she would never have friends who understood. She told me that her mother had been her most loving and toughest teacher. She would send her right back out to play and to learn to fight her own battles with the other children.

Jenny said she learned some things about herself and that she was sometimes tempted to self-pity and sadness. She learned that she could do many things that other children could not do, and that she had many gifts which blindness forced her to discover.

Not long ago I had a letter from Jenny. She is now happily married and is teaching in a school which has several blind students. She wants to share with others the things she has learned about the goodness of life.

Scott: A young man with a learning disability.

When Scott was selected "student of the month" by his teachers at the junior high school where he was then a student, he took the time to tell me some of the story of his life. At age 14, he looked back and was proud when he thought about his past and what might have happened to him.

When he was very young, he had been a hyperactive child. His parents found he was difficult to deal with and other kids didn't want to play with him. When Scott started school, other kids made fun of him and wouldn't invite him to join them.

He explained that he would come home from school, walk up the hill behind his house, lean against his favorite tree, cry and feel very sad. He wondered if he would ever have friends, if others would let him do things with them.

But, he said, the longer he stayed at his favorite spot on the hill and looked out over the valley, the more he thought about his future. He said that he hoped he would be able to help other children with learning disabilities so that they wouldn't have to go through what he had. He didn't want them to feel bad because others rejected them

His learning disability was identified in preschool — one

of the worst they had ever seen, his parents were told. Scott told me that until he was in sixth grade he was still sucking his thumb.

As he began to tell me his dreams for the future, I stopped him and asked, "Scott, who helped you? How did all of this change for you?"

He smiled and said, "My favorite teacher, my second grade teacher. She told me that, even if I had trouble learning, there were many things I could do better than others. She told me that she thought I was a nice person and that she was sure that I could do anything I wanted to do."

To hear Scott talk about his friends, to hear his parents tell about the busy telephone at home, makes the story seem almost unreal. Scott says that the fact that his parents and his teachers encouraged and loved him made the difference. Precisely because he had difficulty learning, he knew he would have to work harder than others. And he had done this.

For the future, he hopes to do something that brings him into contact with others who began as he did so that they can feel as good as he did when he received that school award.

Chris: A child of divorce.

I knew Chris for more than two years, but he had never spoken to me so openly about what his parents' divorce had meant to him. I was deeply moved by both his candor and his caring.

The conversation began one day when he said, "Paula, do you think I could write a book?" Having no idea of what this 10-year-old had in mind, I said, "Well, I guess anyone can write a book who wants to and has something to say."

He got tears in his eyes as he said, "I was 8 years old when my parents were separated. I can remember it was my best year in school. Everything was going the best it had ever gone for me. I was doing well in all of my subjects. I was playing football and having a good time with my friends. Then, my dad moved out and, after that, it seemed as if I lost it all."

He told me that he wasn't very interested in school, that he had a difficult time keeping his mind on his work. Sometimes he just couldn't remember things and his teachers wondered what was wrong. He was afraid to tell them that his parents weren't together anymore.

He described how hurt he felt when he heard some of the kids talking about his parents. One of them even said, "You can't play with us anymore. Your parents are going to get divorced and my mother said that good people don't get divorced."

At first, he couldn't cry at home because he didn't want to hurt either of his parents. He knew that this was hard for them, too. He didn't want the children in school to see him cry so he tried to wait until he was alone somewhere.

"Maybe if I would write a book that would tell other kids who are 8 how it felt for me, then maybe it wouldn't hurt so much for them. Do you think they could learn what would help them if I told them what helped me?"

When I asked Chris who had helped him he said, "My doctor did. When I would go to see him, he told me that I was not too big to cry, that it was all right for boys and men to cry. He told me that most kids my age whose parents get separated are afraid that their parents are going to die. He told me that it wasn't my fault that this happened. He told me that I couldn't feel responsible to try and get my parents back together, even if that was what I really wanted."

As I listened to Chris, his story revealed a number of common denominators of the lives of children of divorce.

He told me about two pictures he drew for his doctor on his first two visits. One was a mask, a very angry face, drawn in red and black. "That's how I felt inside then. I was angry with my parents, with myself, and with everyone." The second picture was of two tall trees without leaves. At the top of each was a tiny nest. Far down below on the ground were four birds. "Now we live in two different houses and neither seems like a place to be anymore."

As he continued to talk about those first few months following the separation, he said again that he wanted to write about how it was to be 8 and, as he said, "To be divorced when you are just 8 years old is hard. I feel sad for any other kids that would ever happen to. Do you think I could help them?"

Some common denominators.

Each has been deeply hurt. They all know what it means to feel pain. And their youth did not make it hurt any less.

Each was missing something that was very important for the future: eyesight, ability to learn as others do, the marriage of parents. Each had experienced some form of rejection by their peers, some painful separation from others.

Each took time to think about what that pain meant. Although young, each was a person of self-reflection. Each wanted to go beyond simply seeing the pain or the loss. Each wanted to come to a place where they could see into what had happened and understand it better.

The presence of another or of others had made the difference for each. Jenny's mother had refused to do for her what tears and tantrums sometimes demanded. Her mother had seen into and beyond the blindness of her daughter so that she might better prepare her for a life that could have meaning and happiness. Scott's teacher had taken time to reassure and to encourage. She had given him the belief that he could have a future life and that he could share his life with others. Chris's doctor helped him to experience and deal with his emotional response to his parents' divorce, and then reassured him that what he was experiencing was normal for someone his age. Helping Chris through this painful time had instilled in the boy a desire to help others his age.

None had any way to run from the painful reality. They saw it, looked at it with someone else and, in a sense, through that person's eyes. Because they did this, they were led from seeing (sight) to insight (seeing some meaning and some common denominators between themselves and others).

After they saw and looked into what had happened, each had a strong motivation to reach out from somewhere deep inside to offer whatever gift each had to another. Their self-reflection nourished by loving support had led each from sight to insight to heartsight.

Self-reflection: Sight, Insight, Heartsight

Sometimes just seeing life as it is requires faith and courage. Simply accepting the givens for life is often more of a challenge than we believe we can accept.

Even at their young ages, Jenny and Scott and Chris had seen. It took courage to reflect on what they had seen, to somehow find meaning in something they would never have chosen. Each manifested personal discipline. Self-reflection is not an easy process; it does not allow one to run away from reality; rather, it leads one into it.

All three had the qualities of a good listener. They listened to their lives and to what was going on around them, and this listening prepared them to listen better to each person who offered them support. Their listening enabled them to share in the insights of others, insights which they might use in the future.

In the most profound sense, Jenny and Scott and Chris were prayerful people. When we are hurting and forced to deal with losses and limitations, we are praying. When we are listening carefully to the call and the encouragement of those who can help us discover our gifts, we are praying. When we are sharing our tears with others in an effort to allow those tears to clear our eyes of obstacles to future life, we are praying. When we are sharing what we have experienced and learned so that others might hurt less or find meaning in their pain, we are praying. When we do these things, we experience one of the fruits of prayer, the gift of heartsight.

Attaining heartsight is the reward for taming our pain; taming it so it belongs to us and not we to it; taming it so that we are not afraid when others have pain because we know that they can tame theirs too, if they are willing to make the effort.

The journey in prayer, the journey with pain, has meaning only if it is shared and only if we are led to a greater desire to share life with others. It is a journey that begins with seeing, passes through insight, and through the mind into the heart.

Obstacles to Seeing With the Heart

These three young people are both hope-filled and happy. They each made the effort to show courage and to be open to life—important factors in their dealing with pain-filled situations.

We and they might "miss our lives as they come at us," as Wallace Stegner suggests. We might fail to be present to them at any given moment. And we might not seek the meaning which is important in giving direction to the future.

To learn the secret of the fox in *The Little Prince* — "It is only with the heart that one can see rightly; what is essential is invisible to the eye" — we must remove from our hearts and lives all those things that obscure or prevent seeing. These obstacles to seeing with the heart are also the obstacles to accepting and cultivating prayer as a way of both seeing and living.

Some obstacles to prayer are:

—Our refusal to accept the givens of our lives. There were things in the lives of Jenny, Scott and Chris that they did not cause and could not change. Life for them meant dealing with what they could not remove.

—Our refusal to listen carefully to the truth of our lives and to the experience of others.

—Our failure to pursue the discovery of our gifts and to use those we already realize.

—Our contentment with superficiality, with discovering only a small portion of life's truth and possibilities. Our contentment with living only on the outside of our lives.

—Our fear of looking into our lives and taking time to reflect on their meaning, lest the demands increase as we are called to more life.

—Our hunch that we are called to life by a God who will continue to prod us when we are willing to settle for less.

—Our propensity to put things off, to plan to take time later, to wait until we are less tired or tried.

—Our failure to realize that only those things inside of us can ever, finally, destroy us or bring us to greater life.

—Our avoidance of the solitude required for the messages of life to pass from the outside in.

—Our quest for just the right subject matter and our avoidance of distraction. We forget that whatever is in our hearts and important to our lives is appropriate when we come before the Lord.

—Our preoccupation with methods of prayer. Sometimes continually searching for the sure "how to pray" method may simply be a manifestation of our procrastination.

I remember a retreat master who once said that he would teach us a never-fail method of praying. He said, "It is my method of 'Meditating by Distraction.'" He went on to encourage us to take the fabric of our lives, each thread and each color, each image and each space, and to center our prayer on them. "The subject matter of life," he said, "is the subject matter of our prayer."

That's what Jenny and Scott and Chris did. They took

the threads of their own tapestries and found new meaning and new life in them.

Following God's Lead in Prayer

A friend told me that she was visiting her sister's home shortly before Christmas. Her favorite nephew, 5-year-old Danny, was playing in a corner of the living room.

She asked him if he had written his letter to Santa Claus. He kept on playing and she was not certain that he had heard her question. So she asked him again, "Have you written your letter to Santa yet?"

He looked at her, said nothing, but shook his head no. She was puzzled and then, thinking that he could not write, thought he might like some help. When she offered to help him write to Santa, he told her that he was not going to write a letter.

Fearing that he might have heard something about Santa from his 9-year-old sister, she asked him, "Don't you believe in Santa?" His answer was simple and direct, "Yes, I believe in Santa. He has always been good to me."

Now my friend was both puzzled and curious so she asked, "Will you tell me why you don't want to write a letter to Santa?"

Danny's response was not long in coming. He explained, "I don't want to write to Santa because if I write and tell him all the things I want, I'll never know what he just wanted to give me."

What a wonderful commentary on the only form of prayer that many of us use consistently — telling God what we need and asking him to give it to us. Certainly, St. Paul was right when he said, "The Spirit too comes to help us in our weakness, for, when we do not know how to pray properly, then the Spirit personally makes our petitions" (Rom 8:26).

Like ourselves, the followers of Jesus complained that

they did not know how to pray. They knew that Jesus took time apart, that he needed the moments of solitude to listen carefully to the inner movements in his life and to give direction to the life that he shared so well with others.

We know that when his closest followers asked him how to pray he taught them the Lord's Prayer. Jesus was inviting them to much more than the recitation of set words. He wanted them to include the elements of prayer that are clearly set in the model prayer that he gave them.

When we pray, we, like Jesus, are to approach God as Abba — as father, as mother, as friend, as loving presence. We come before God in a stance of loving familiarity and hope-filled acceptance. We come with the belief that the relationship between ourselves and God is undeserved but can never be lost.

To come before God as a familiar and loving presence presumes that we have the faith which Paul Tillich defined as "accepting God's acceptance." So, even to say the first words of the Lord's Prayer is to give credence and expression to an established and trusted bond between ourselves and God.

The greater our awareness that God is always with us, the more confidently we will pray that his kingdom will come on earth, in us, in those we love, in all.

To pray that the kingdom may come in us gives us the responsibility to remove obstacles in ourselves which prevent our involvement in our own lives, obstacles which block our ability to hear God's loving and persistent call in every event of life.

Revelation is here and now. God's presence in our lives is revealed in and through the persons, events, and circumstances of our daily lives. When we ask that the kingdom may come, we are asking that we may be more aware of and come to better understand the many ways in which God is already present in our lives. We also ask that we may be prepared to receive God's presence in future events.

We pray, in the Lord's Prayer, that God's coming may extend into our world so that all men and women may notice and acknowledge that God's loving presence is revealed in our relationships. God is revealed in the efforts of reconciliation between persons as well as nations.

Because we recognize some of our own obstacles to God's coming into our lives, we pray for forgiveness. We ask to be healed and strengthened so that we may be forgiven and that we may forgive ourselves and one another.

None of us can withhold our forgiveness until someone else has forgiven. The responsibility for the first steps toward healing lie with the person courageous enough to presume to use the words of the prayer Jesus gave us.

We are called to love and forgive with the same unconditional love and unqualified care that God offers us. This is not a negotiable item when we pray. God loves us too much to allow us to offer less than all and he accepts every effort on our part to remove the things that interfere with this kind of loving and forgiving.

Finally, in the Lord's Prayer we pray not only for the coming of the kingdom here on earth but we offer praise to God because the "power and the kingdom and the glory" are God's and must be recognized and loved because they are his.

Because something in us instinctively and mysteriously refuses to let God in, this element of prayer is most difficult and most costly for us. Something in us says "no" to the coming of God's kingdom, "no" to the inbreaking of life.

To pray for the coming of the kingdom in the world is to seek not only the removal of obstacles in our lives and hearts but to be an instrument ready to prepare for the coming of the kingdom for all. It is to offer a commitment to reach back out from our hearts and from the vision of life we have found there to touch into the lives of others.

To pray, as we do, "For yours is the kingdom and the power and the glory," is to make a commitment beyond seeing, beyond seeing into. It is a commitment to see and hear with the heart and to share with others what we discover in prayer.

Heartsight: A Gift We Offer to Others

When we take the time and make the effort to pray, we grow in our realization that there is much more to our lives than ourselves. Each effort to come before a God of love to seek healing and wholeness allows the kingdom to come in us and prepare us for its coming in the world.

When we reach out of the deepest recesses of our hearts, sometimes hurting and sometimes joy-filled, our vision grows larger and our gifts grow stronger. In the act of reaching out, our hearts are expanded beyond what we ever might have dreamed possible.

When we are frightened and feel vulnerable to what surrounds us, we are called, sometimes beyond our own wills, to deepen our commitment to develop our talents and to allow those gifts to flow over into those with whom we share life.

People who do not pray are not likely to hear life as it comes at them. They are not likely to reflect on its meaning even after it has passed.

The life of a person who does not seek solitude and self-reflection is like a painting by a painter who is incapable of creating depth and perspective. Just as the painting will appear one-dimensional, so will the lack of depth of a nonpraying person become apparent.

The praying person is one who walks in the awareness of the human condition and the reality of both its gifts and limitations. Such a person will be an affirming, caring and challenging presence to others.

The vision of heartsight is knowing that we will not always walk in consolation and freedom from pain, even though we are invited to be on familiar terms with God. We cherish God's love precisely because we are sometimes pain-laden and filled with doubts. To expect that the God who calls us to love and forgive will shield us from anguish is to misunderstand the purpose of prayer.

Heartsight is a vision of life born of pain, tension, seeking and risking. It is a vision that enables us to be present to ourselves now, a vision that accepts God as revealed in the lives of others. Heartsight is what we seek in prayer, what we nourish with prayer.

12 Remembering to Give Back

Isn't it a pity,
Forgetting to give back.

George Harrison

Remembering is part of what makes us human. It reminds us that life is about giving and receiving. It gives direction to our lives.

The story of Mr. Singer in Carson McCullers' *The Heart Is a Lonely Hunter* is about remembering and forgetting. It is the story of a man who noticed what was important to the lives of others and then remembered to be a part of bringing it to them.

Singer is a deaf mute who tenderly cares for a mentally retarded friend. When the friend is institutionalized, Singer remembers to bring him the things he loves — the things he likes to eat, the things that will make him happy. He is the lonely retarded man's only friend.

Singer also lives with a family that has a teenage daughter. He brings happiness to her also by playing the music she likes in his room (though he cannot hear) and by sharing happy times at places like the circus.

Singer befriends a black doctor whose daughter seems to have abandoned him and the doctor turns to Singer to help him make peace with his daughter.

This deaf mute, who hears the music of life and sees the goodness in the lives of others, gives to all. He remembers the special needs of others and forgets his own loneliness. It is only after his tragic suicide that those he remembered so well come to realize that they did not remember him, that they did not notice his hurts, his needs, his wants. One of them commented, "We all needed him. We never remembered to think of his needs." The forgotten man had not failed to remember others.

His story is a reminder of the relationship between remembering and forgetting. It is about giving and receiving. It is about responses that give and sometimes give back.

Sharing and Remembering

When Jesus was sharing his final meal with his friends, he began by giving thanks. Then he blessed both the cup and the bread and asked that his final sharing, blessing and thanksgiving be repeated in his memory.

> Then, taking a cup, he gave thanks and said, "Take this and share it among you, because from now on, I tell you, I shall never again drink wine until the kingdom of God comes."
>
> Then he took bread, and when he had given thanks, he broke it and gave it to them, saying, "This is my body given for you; do this in remembrance of me." He did the same with the cup after supper, and said, "This cup is the new covenant in my blood poured out for you" (Lk 22:17-20).

Giving thanks, blessing, sharing and remembering are the fundamental requirements for the followers of Jesus. The celebration of the last supper is a celebration of the first meal of thanksgiving and commitment, the meal that called us to be a eucharistic people. In this meal Jesus invites his closest friends and his followers through the centuries to remember his life, his faithfulness to his Father, his responsive love for those around him, his courageous life that led to his death.

To share in the Eucharist is to remember how, and the

conditions under which, Jesus offered it to his friends. He extended the challenging invitation to be a people who offer our broken lives as we seek God's blessing, to be a people who choose a direction that will mean pouring out our lives. He asks that we do this with the same faithfulness and unqualified love he offers us.

To commit ourselves to understand the words and actions of Jesus involves stripping away some historical accumulations, some forms of heresy, some legalistic interpretations of the meaning of sign and sacrament. When we do this, we come face to face with questions about thanksgiving, blessing, sharing and remembering — questions to which Jesus invites us now as he invited his friends then.

Giving thanks first, as Jesus did, prepares us well to remember the good gifts and the painful aggravations of each day. Out of a stance toward life that manifests gratitude, we pray for blessing as we recall blessings already received.

Bread broken and shared in the Eucharist is not like a consoling form of sweet roll; rather, it is like whole grain bread of rich and unrefined texture. A God who loves us and the Lord who leads us care too much to offer only the promise of childlike contentment and protection. The memorial of Jesus includes both the celebration of Passover and the suffering of Good Friday. Each has more meaning because of the other. Each prepares us for the new life of Easter Sunday. To claim as our own the whole grain bread that is life-like and hope-sustaining is to be faithful to the memorial of Jesus.

> The dripping blood our only drink,
> The bloody flesh our only food:
> In spite of which we like to think
> That we are sound, substantial flesh and blood—
> Again, in spite of that, we call this Friday good.
>
> *East Coker,* T.S. Eliot

To share the Eucharist and to remember its meaning is to see that forgiveness is a prerequisite for us as it was for Jesus in relationship to Judas. Our remembering will lead to the scene where Jesus' friends abandoned him — friends who had earlier shared the lovingly blessed and freely offered bread and cup from their friend and companion.

To approach that bread and cup demands that we seek to remove from our hearts and our lives whatever interferes with being forgiving people as a part of the memorial to which we are invited each time we approach the table of the Lord.

Jesus did not remain at the table. He went out to pray and prepare himself for the horrors that were soon to follow. He took with him his most trusted friends, the closest three. He led them to a place where he was unprotected and available to the wiles of his betrayer and the angry soldiers.

To share the cup and break the bread is to see availability to others as a necessary ingredient of faithfulness to the life we seek. This is no subtle reminder, but a dramatic proclamation of the price that presence to others may exact from us. Jesus offered the bread and the cup to his friends after he had offered prayers of thanks and blessing. Each was given as gift to his followers, without selectivity or condition.

All too often we have treated the bread of life as reward rather than gift. We have become selective about who may receive it. We have dared to set conditions on what Jesus offered unconditionally.

If Jesus had offered the cup and the bread as reward for conformity or for perfect faithfulness, either in relationship to those who shared that meal with him or to us, few could remain at the table.

Reclaiming the invitation to share the loving gift of the cup and the bread frees us to approach with gratitude a Lord who calls us to become more like him, but does not send us away empty when our pursuit of Christian ideals is less than perfect.

Remembering that table where the cup and bread were blessed reminds us that sharing is risky business. The man who left that table to cry out to his Father in the garden and later from the cross does not claim to lead us to some secure harbor where we can hide and live untroubled lives.

The invitation to give thanks for the sharing and the remembering asks of us the same self-involvement and marginal living characteristic of those who follow his way. The call to give thanks and bless in memory of him is Jesus' certain way of demanding some return for the good gifts we have received. Faithfulness to the memorial of Jesus is not possible if we forget to sometimes give back.

Giving Back — In Memory of Him

Thanking, blessing and remembering are not simple commitments. Each is demanding. Each is self-involving. Each can involve risking. When we do these things, we are led to live and to give according to gifts received and efforts to remember.

The memorial of Jesus will not allow us to simply give some of what we have. The remembering is not complete unless we share who we are on our journey. The call of Jesus to remember is not an invitation to either stumble around in the past or to settle down in it and live out our lives. Those who follow Jesus bear a responsibility to be mindful of the past, to live in the present and to give direction to the future.

Looking back is important. It helps us to realize and see now what we might have missed. We do this to redeem our past, to avoid repeating its mistakes. In the light of the past, but not cowering in its shadow, we grow more present to each day's life. We cherish the experiences that have been ours as we celebrate the truth we have discovered and the wisdom we have acquired.

With confidence that we are present to and involved in each day's living, we trust whatever the darkness or uncertainty may hide from us.

Jesus remembered and celebrated the life he had shared

with Judas as well as with John and Peter. The many meals he had shared with a small group of friends and with the crowds gathered on the hillsides were not initiated by selective invitation. So, too, with this final passover meal.

Part of our giving back as we seek to remember what Jesus said and did is to become more aware of the many hungers of the human family — an awareness of the hungers of the body and spirit that is necessary to be involved in the memorial.

We respond with blessing and thanks to an increased awareness of the many forms of nourishment essential to the fullest human life. When we respond with open and sometimes empty hands and hearts, we resemble the Jesus in the garden asking the Father to remove his suffering; we resemble the Jesus on the cross crying out with anguished complaint that the Father has abandoned him.

When we remember to give back, we discover that no gift is ever given for ourselves alone as no suffering was meant to be borne in isolation. All is given to us so that it might be poured out and blessed in the very process of being shared.

Sharing the Direction of Our Lives

The message of the Christian gospel and the story of human history reveal that men and women were not meant to live in isolation. In sharing the experiences of our personal lives and the events of history we set the course of each of us as well as the direction of human evolution.

In an interview in *Newsweek* magazine, Mircea Eliade stated, "The history of religion shows that we are not just biological cousins of the aboriginals, but friends and collaborators in a common human enterprise."

He comments further that the enemies of this new humanistic synthesis are the theologians who want to demythologize religion and the secularists who try to explain away religion as being merely the product of the unconscious, or of a set of social processes.

Religion that is true to the God who is revealed through its questioning is at the heart of the human quest for life and meaning. It cannot be separated from the sociological processes that surround it. Religious experience is rooted in the full spectrum of life through which God is revealed.

Teilhard de Chardin, in his writings about the future of the human person and the capacity of each to develop psychologically and physically, reminds us of the power and the ability of the human species to decide what kind of people we will become and to determine how we will share this process with one another. More than 50 years ago he spoke prophetically of "world community."

Setting Jesus at the center of human evolution, he proclaimed that shared love is basic to any form of life in the cosmos. He issued a strong challenge in *Building the Earth* to develop the relational nature of human life not as an option but as a necessity for life together on this planet.

Love is the most universal, formidable and mysterious of cosmic energies. From the point of view of Spiritual Evolution, it seems that we might be able to give a new name and a value to this strange energy of love.

He declares that the age of individualistic nations is past and if we are to survive, our task is to divest ourselves of ancient and paralyzing prejudices.

The basic commitment of our baptism is to share life, to offer support and care to one another along the way. Fulfilling this commitment rests in remembering that we are nourished in and through the process of sharing.

Being Broken and the Emergence of Life

We are sometimes reluctant followers of Jesus. Too often he leads us where we would rather not go. He cares for others with a kind of love that both challenges and cherishes, an art that we learn only with great difficulty.

Following Jesus seems easy when we think of him with the large and affirming crowds, when we remember the procession of palms into the city of Jerusalem.

Following Jesus is attractive when we read of the blind man given sight and the young daughter of Jairus who was brought back to life.

Like the apostles and closest friends of Jesus, we may be surprised at our own cowardice when the crowds are hostile and the soldiers are leading him away. Like them, we want to run away to some safer place and to some easier teacher.

When Jesus gives thanks, blesses and shares the meal with his friends, the images of bread broken and wine poured take on a meaning that has direct implications for those who choose to remember and follow in his way.

The image of breaking is closely associated with the emergence of

— The freezing rain and ice which seep into large rocks and, through weathering, help form new soil in which new life can grow.

— The protective coats of dormant seeds which are broken through so the tiny embryo can contact the nourishing soil and moisture.

— Tiny roots which sometimes break through hardened soil in their need for minerals and water.

— Clouds which break open and return their water to a nurturing earth.

— The umbilical cord which must be broken, severed, so that independent life can begin.

— Bonds which are broken with the familiar in life's transitions.

— Adolescents who wrestle with and eventually break the bonds with their parents in order to form stronger and more appropriate bonds for the life they seek.

—The structures of society which break so that new forms may emerge.

—Hearts which sometimes painfully break because of rejection and failed friendships, offering the possibility of freeing people to learn how to love one another.

Breaking, like the death of Jesus, precedes new life. The meaning of the breaking of the bread at that final meal, neither began nor ended there.

Jesus told his followers in ways sometimes too straightforward to hear, that if they wanted to remain his friends, they would have to walk the way he walked. They would have to eat his flesh and make his values their own if they wanted to bear the name Christian as his memorial.

When the crowds gathered on the hillside and the apostles came to tell him of their hunger, they did not expect his answer. Instead of sending them away to the villages to buy their own food, Jesus reminded them that giving and sharing what we have is required of us.

> When evening came, the disciples went to him and said, "This is a lonely place, and the time has slipped by; so send the people away, and they can go to the villages to buy themselves some food." Jesus replied, "There is no need for them to go: give them something to eat yourselves" (Mt 14:15-16).

Their complaints about how little food they had could not change his simple injunction, "Feed them." Jesus took for granted sharing and blessing each other in the act of hospitality.

Throughout his life, Jesus said and did things which involved misunderstanding, criticism and even hostility in his relationships with others. Because he took it for granted that pain was a part of life and that suffering was a companion, it is not surprising that, in those final moments of sharing, he

would repeat this reminder to his friends: When you remember me, remember also that this bread has been broken and
this wine poured out. At that moment, all lives that would
ever be broken in the process of sharing life were blessed and
offered by Jesus. And, thanks were given.

Sharing Life as an Act of Thankfulness

Even in those final moments at the passover meal he so
much wanted to share, the signs of the times had made it apparent to Jesus that his enemies were not few. In those final
moments, he remembered that his way of living and the quality of his loving had made powerful enemies. Yet in the face of
this, he chose to gather with his friends and celebrate the
friendship and life they shared, to give thanks and to offer
blessings.

The greatest meaning of suffering is revealed when we
share it with others as a gift we have received. The pain involved in self-discovery, by which we come to cherish ourselves, prepares us to offer the gift of ourselves to another.

Reverencing the gifts of others and our own is not easily
learned. Most often we learn it by painful trial and error.

Like the apostles and the hungry people on the hillside,
we come with only a few loaves and fishes in our lives. In the
end, like the people in that gathering, we leave with much
more than what we had in the beginning. That's the nature of
sharing.

At the last meal, Jesus leaves his most profound message
through his example. It is as though he needs some final way
to say "thank you" to those with whom he had shared his
greatest joys and most profound pain. Each important action
begins with first giving thanks and then offering a blessing.
What begins with thanksgiving and blessing ends in the act of
sharing.

For us, as for those gathered with Jesus, giving thanks
and sharing are not meant ever to be separated. What we receive with gratitude we are called to freely share:

As the chosen of God, then, the holy people whom he loves, you are to be clothed in heartfelt compassion, in generosity and humility, gentleness and patience. . . . And may the peace of Christ reign in your hearts, because it is for this that you were called together in one body. Always be thankful (Col 3:12, 15).